PEACEFULLY CENTERED

PEACEFULLY CENTERED

A Guide to Spiritual Serenity

Nicole Quatela

Dedication

This dedication belongs to my sister in Christ; my Michelle. Michelle is a person of intense passion, who delights in expressing her warm, genuine love for others, wherever her travels take her. She is a person of great distinction, who continues to search for God, in everything she does. Michelle fills others with happiness and joy, because she herself is filled with exuberance. She often allows us to receive her wonderful gift of optimism, which she gives with a solid dose of realism. It truly pleases her to counsel and provide me with substantive solutions to my problems. Michelle, I have closely listened to the wisdom which you have imparted, and by embodying all of the good qualities which The Holy Spirit has given you, you are then able to sustain the glorious relationship, which you experience with our Higher Power. The time you spend in seclusion with God is the most significant act that you perform during your day. As a result, many people benefit from your reverent prayers and your meaningful readings. Michelle, you are undeniably my most treasured friend, and I cannot ever envision you leaving the very special place you hold in my heart. So then, thank you for your invaluable friendship, for meeting me where I happen to be, and for the way you inspire me every day.

Preface

Before I started writing *Peacefully Centered*, I found that my faith was completely enmeshed in my life, even though I had not taken the time to reflect upon the contents of my beliefs. As I started to explore what my beliefs embodied, God Himself revealed some intriguing Truths to me, which I documented in this book. As I learned the intimacy of these fascinating Truths, they were responsible for energizing my faith, as I believed that these Truths were a gift given to me because of my curiosity for all things spiritual. Even though there were numerous spiritual concepts which I could have added to my belief system, I ultimately decided to align myself with ideologies that my intuition affirmed. This book may offer you answers to some of your spiritual inquiries, and it may also encourage you to engage in a journey, which may gently guide you towards your inner peace. It is my hope that this book will serve you well, especially if you wish to pursue a more profound spirituality, and wish to build a stronger connection with our Higher Power.

Table of Contents

Declarations

'As it is written' which has either been placed prior to or subsequent to a quotation, signifies that the quote is from The New American Bible, Saint Joseph Edition.

Each time 'Our Higher Power' is written, and issues are discussed which come from The New Testament, you should understand that our Higher Power's intentions are executed through His Son.

The phrase, 'The Entities of the Complete Being' is used in place of the Holy Trinity, since this will help the readers understand that the Entities can be separate from one another, at times.

The prince of darkness is the devil; however, the dark force includes the devil and his dark angels.

Words or phrases encapsulated by "quotation marks," such as these, signify that these words are found in the Bible, and the whole quote may be researched by using the catalogue of quotes, in the back of the book.

These 'quotation marks' are used for emphasis, for a distinction of sorts, or quotes words from others, which are not from The New American Bible, Saint Joseph Edition.

Chapter 1: Peacefully Centered

Peacefully Centered is a wonderfully fulfilling journey, which occurs when we decide to supplement our spiritual beliefs, with non-conflicting additional beliefs, so that we enable ourselves to feel whole and excited about our faith. This journey may occur throughout our lives, usually by assessing one belief at a time, as we will choose a new and an essential answer to each of the questions or issues that are presented. Our choice should concur with our intuition in the end. This allows each of us to create a unique core religion, which will suit us in a more purposeful way, and therefore, ideologies that satisfy our intuition, should be added to our faith. Our intuition comes to us from our Higher Power, and we shall reap these intuitive benefits when we: converse with Him and His Son, read various books concerning other belief-systems, attend a variety of religious services, and gather knowledge from other faith-driven people. What possesses us to make one decision, over another? Simply put, it is our intuition, which nudges us towards the right decision for each of us. As we recognize, understand, and add some fresh, yet unfamiliar beliefs to our faith, this will strengthen the intensity of our bond with our Higher Power. He wants us to delve into the spiritual world, and create a special religion where each of us can worship Him, in the best possible way. If we are willing to relax our own minds, so that we open ourselves to a world of diversity and unique ideas, we will in turn have the ability to shift our attention towards the practice of spiritual fluidity. Spiritual fluidity consists of religious concepts that travel into or out of our consciousness, as we test them for possible answers to frequently asked questions, depending on if the concept resonates with our intuition. One of these new spiritual concepts may find their way into our faith, even today, as we slowly build our faith, one belief at a time. We will find complete tranquility within our spiritual life, when we start to experience all of the harmony, which has led us to a variety of spiritual beliefs. This will motivate us to converse with our Higher Power even more, as He will guide us through situations in which we may glean some astonishing glimpses, into His love for us. Our enlightenment will begin to flow, as our newly born revelations are a testament to His love and concern for us. As it is written, "There are in the end three things that last: faith, hope, and love, and the greatest of these is love." If you are indeed *Peacefully Centered*, you will have no doubts in what you believe and trust, as love will have become your spiritual truth. As we walk along the path of our centeredness, these steps shall lead us to share the love we have for others. We will develop more love for our Higher Power, His Son, and as a result, there will be more love for our neighbors, as love becomes the most significant discovery, within our inner peace. Scripture dictates how love is translated, as it elegantly appears in the New Testament. "Love is patient; love is kind. Love is not jealous, it does not put on airs, it is not snobbish. Love is never rude, it is not self-seeking, it is not prone to anger; neither does it brood over injuries. Love does not rejoice in what is wrong but rejoices within the truth. There is no limit to love's forbearance, to its trust, its hope, its power to endure," as it is written. When we learn to genuinely love others, we will find ourselves seeking our Higher Power within each and every person we meet. As we pass this love onto others, the desire we have to assist our neighbors, simply becomes a fulfillment of what He has asked of us. We become the one who will gladly serve others, as our centeredness comes full circle. Our Higher Power's love blesses us, as we pass these blessings onto others, and as a result we ourselves become peaceful. Our spirituality flourishes, as our love blossoms and continuously grows. When we make life easier for others, we make life more enjoyable for ourselves. In order to be *Peacefully Centered*, we should essentially envelop our fellow man with comforting words, as he will experience an ease and a serenity within himself, when we spend time together during an environment of gentleness and consideration for one another. If we took the time to spread the wealth of our compassion, which The Holy Spirit has bestowed upon each of us, there would not be the unnecessary prejudices nor the abuses we hear of daily. Simply speaking kindly to others may be a lost art, since we have deprived ourselves of the ability to see our Higher

Power in each other. This breeds a lack of respect, and a lack of consideration which each of us has for one another. We should not become mentally engaged, nor entangled with the affairs of this life; such as trying to get even with the individual who previously hurt us. We are finite beings, since our outer shells have a beginning and an end, however, we become infinite beings through our souls, as our essence travels to an afterlife. Since we are not aware of the date nor the time of our death, let us always remain within the grasp of our Higher Power and His Son, by continuing to converse with them, and continuing to do what satisfies them. As it is written, "The Son of Man is coming at the time you least expect,"; "Stay awake, therefore! You cannot know the day your Lord is coming,"; "As for the exact day or hour, no one knows it, neither the angels in heaven nor the Son, but the Father only." The Almighty has not given us the privilege of comprehending His omnipotent ways, however, our Higher Power intimates that we will learn some of these methods, possibly through His Son during our afterlife. Join me now, as we continue to explore the various answers, which will be presented in a progression of chapters, as they were created by a variety of novel ideas, which came to me from God Himself. Let us ponder these thoughts, as we shall be responsible for adding that information to our beliefs; however, only if this knowledge agrees with our intuition. You will experience the beautiful blossoming of love through these fresh spiritual ideas, as we start on the path to being *Peacefully Centered.*

Chapter 2: One Higher Power

There is exclusively one God, who ultimately creates the thoughts and actions we execute. As it is written, "There are different gifts, but the same spirit, there are different ministries but the same Lord, there are different works, but the same God, who accomplishes all of them in everyone." If we happen to belong to another world religion, other than Christianity, I humbly believe that our Higher Power chooses to answer everyone's prayers, as He knows the hearts of all who pray. It does not matter how we choose to celebrate our love for Him, however, it is that we choose to celebrate, by praying to Him with sincere and virtuous intentions. It is certainly meaningful, that our Higher Power lives within us, however, this does not signify that we are spiritually and emotionally bonded to Him, as both parties must invariably communicate together, so that our conversation may help us form an intimate relationship with each other. At first, God oversees the actions we commit, such as He did with Adam's sinful bite of the apple. He observed the sin Adam perpetrated, as He generously granted each of us a free will to act in the manner we wish, which can sometimes distance us from God. Subsequently, in order to impede our flesh-driven sins, we can ask Him to be the helmsman of our ship, which places our lives in God's hands. Our Higher Power does not wish to truly control our lives, however, He will protect us and guide us, by sending helpful messages to our intuition and to our mind, which will suggest that we should avoid sin at all times, even though we continue to possess a free will. The question becomes, 'Will we continue to follow Him, even though we have a free will?' Let us remember that He will forever hold us, and envelop us with His comforting arms, no matter what we choose to do with our free will. When I picture our Higher Power in my consciousness, I imagine an Entity, who exists everywhere. Our Higher Power acts as a highly organized quantum of unknown energy, as He slowly swirls and lingers about and through every one of us. He performs this act with the intensity of a deliberate wind.

He remains this particular way, so that He may continue to be cognizant of any and all information concerning us; and by being around and through us, He can truly envelop and love each one of us, at the same time. Our Higher Power's existence is not based on segmented intervals of duration, which is how we choose to keep track of our existence. We have become so attentive to the clock, and to the yearly calendar, so that we can make sense of our lives. He experiences all matters within the present, as He remains ageless, and exists in a timeless domain. He perpetually exists, and time cannot be documented properly by utilizing our system of time intervals, since He has no beginning and no end. Each of us tends to speculate upon the Theory of Creationism, since we do not have a firm grasp of how long it took for each one of the seven days to elapse. This conundrum becomes a loose guess at best. I believe that as long as we live in the present, we will certainly live within His presence. He knows the future; however, He lives in the present so that He can assist us, and create differences in our lives. When we ask for our Higher Power's help and direction, it may seem as though He does not always answer us, however, at times, when we are not searching for Him, and we need Him most of all, He will be there to lovingly support us. As we continuously move into the physical present, with each tick of the clock, we understand that we should also cognitively live in the present. 'Carpe diem,' as we do not know if we will live to see another glorious day. This book embraces the concepts, which I believe pleases our Higher Power, and therefore, my hope is that you will use this guide as a starting point, as you commence to form your own beliefs, which will help widen the scope of your core faith. At times, we begin to be absorbed by useless details from within our own religion, as we tend to forget the bigger picture and the more important messages, which are the messages of hope, love, and faith. I am aware that being *Peacefully Centered* is unique to every one of us, as each of us will hold onto our own special faith. I find that most religions strike a genuine resemblance to the Christian religions, and that all religions basically possess similar belief systems. For instance, I humbly believe that the Buddhist's gentle, yet passionate prayers are received by our Higher Power, who then reflects upon these spiritual requests, and responds to a Buddhist's prayer, just as He would acknowledge a Christian's prayer, since Buddhists and Christians often pray for the same meaningful petitions, as do people of other religions. Buddhism is a beautiful religion. For instance, the way in which peace is understood, begins with the 3 pillars of relationship: 1. Our relationship with God, 2. Our relationship with nature, and 3. Our relationship with others. In Christianity, however, there remains one incomparable action of unconditional love, which Jesus endured for us. This is how the Christian religions differentiate themselves, from all other religions of the world. Jesus has and will continue to eternally save the lives of our souls, as all Christians firmly believe. Since we acknowledge this to be our Truth, the ultimate faith we have in Him, demonstrates that His death will lead to our soul's eternal life, as Christianity is life itself. Non-Christians, however, cannot comprehend the profoundness of Jesus' love for us, as He represents the beauty of our faith, and the essence of each of our beliefs. I cannot comprehend, however, that our Higher Power or Jesus would ever punish those of us who are non-Christians for practicing our own faith; especially when we are born into another religion, and continue to live our lives with strong morals, in a faith other than Christianity. I humbly believe, that if we remain well-intentioned, virtuous individuals by: showing concern for ourselves and others, and having a faith which we carefully follow and vigorously believe in, then our soul shall be with God upon our demise. Jesus will judge us by the strength of our faith, regardless of which non-Christian religion has inspired some of us. Therefore, as it is written, "I assure you, whatever you declare bound on earth shall be held bound in heaven, and whatever you declare loosed on earth shall be held loosed in heaven." The significance of this quote is explained in chapter 30, and its meaning verifies the Truth which He has disclosed to me, and I have, in turn, disclosed to you. When we continue to stretch our minds, and increase our knowledge base, we continue to improve our comprehension of whom He is as a Being, and how He actually exists among us. I do not mean to describe 'Being' in the sense of a person, however, I do mean Being in the sense of: An Existence in perpetuity, the Originator and Source of the universe and beyond, and the

Creator of life and of humanity. Let us not forget the two human beings, which He formed with His hands, as we are all descendants of Adam and Eve, and not of animals. We should feel our internal smile, when we think or speak of His love for us, as He is a comforting presence in our life, and He wants us to enjoy ourselves when we are with Him. Our Higher Power possesses a transcending life force, which He bestows upon all of us. This energy comes to us when we make a commitment to be one of His earthly disciples. As our spirituality blossoms, there is one Higher Power, so that the persuasion or denomination of our faith is not so important, as is our love for Him. Once we sustain a love for our Higher Power, He will then lead us to the concepts to which He espouses. Let us allow a few fresh notions to assimilate into our core religion, which will accommodate our particular personality and belief-system, as our fresh opinions regarding these notions will help us to further flourish in our own faith. Therefore, let us cast our nets widely, as various ideas, which come from: God Himself, other religions, and other sources, will be caught within these nets, when we each pursue His calling, which consists of spending more time in passionate and profound conversation with Him, concerning our newly-found spiritual material.

Chapter 3: Why Are We Here?

Most of us are curious regarding why we were chosen to be born on this planet. I humbly believe that we are not only here to serve our Higher Power and honor His wishes, but we are also here, in order to enjoy a source of love and companionship with Him and with our neighbors. Our Higher Power is not pleased at first, due to all of our iniquities, however, later in our Sacred Scripture, during the New Testament, He becomes content with us, as we are His greatest achievement. He delights in all of the experiences He gives us, and looks forward to the more intimate time we shall have, when we meet Him in the afterlife. Our life on earth, must prepare us for our eternal reward. Our reward completely depends upon being adjudicated by His merciful Son, as He considers the genuine feelings we possess, concerning the strength of our faith. Before Jesus has a chance to judge us, let us, with a repentant heart, ask Him for His absolution each time we sin. Personally, I request His forgiveness every night, prior to the time I go to sleep. Our soul was first and foremost created in Heaven, and then placed inside of us by our Higher Power's gentle hands, just as we were being born into this world. I wonder why He did not allow our souls to remain in Heaven with Him, where we could have been an immediate source of companionship? If we had remained with our Maker in Heaven, we would have never encountered some of the same tests and trappings which Jesus experienced. As a result, we have had the chance to empathize with Christ and His temptations, therefore, we must remain on earth for some time, where God can see the strength of our faith, and gauge the power of our love, when we encounter various circumstances and situations on earth. By each of us living on earth, He has granted us the ability to recognize, and understand what it is like to be enticed and sin against God. As a result, most of us accept and relish the moment, that we will someday be in Heaven with our Higher Power, where there is no more suffering of any kind. The choices we make for our lives, are of interest to Him, since we utilize the free will, He has given us. Our Higher Power has decided to bestow a rare and remarkable gift unto each of us, as this gift will give us the ability to develop a spiritual identity, which will then leave an imprint upon our souls, and His Son shall use this imprint to judge us accordingly. We should begin to fathom that our souls are in fact alive for the remainder of eternity, as we belong to our Higher Power forever. We cannot escape this fact, nor should we wish to, if we continue to prepare ourselves properly for the afterlife. Our essence will eventually be released from our bodies, as His Son shall call our soul over to Himself upon our demise. I humbly believe that upon our demise, we will continuously have the desire to be with our Higher Power, as we know that He has the same desire for us. This love and desire from our Higher Power and His Son will be the greatest gift, that we could ever have been granted. As it is written in Genesis, "See! The man has become like one of us, knowing what is good and what is bad! Therefore, he must not be allowed to put out his hand to take fruit from the tree of life, also, and thus eat of it and live forever." This quote states that God does not want us to live forever, just yet. I understand that our Higher Power does not wish for us to die, and thereby live as an essence, solely by eating fruit from the tree of life. By doing so, we would instantly benefit by living in an afterlife forever, at a moment which is unfavorable to our Higher Power, since He has given each of us a wondrous life to live on earth, prior to us living anywhere else. Even though we will depart into the afterlife as sinners, we will eventually become absolved of all of our sins, as we will first need to be admitted into a specialized location called the temporary premises, which will either be physical or cognitive in nature, prior to our souls entering into Heaven within the arms of Jesus. We will all be cleansed at this specialized location by His Son's merciful forgiveness, as our souls will eventually materialize and appear without imperfection, from the temporary premises. This is how Jesus saved our souls; He absolved us of our sins so that we could be given our eternal reward in Heaven with the Entities of the Complete Being. A sin occurs when we fail to do what is right according to Jesus' New Covenant, which signifies that we have either rebelled, at least in part, against our Higher Power, His Son, and/or

The Holy Spirit. The word covenant here suggests a pact, a promise, or a stipulation, which He created between Himself and us. Nothing, throughout human history, has any other individual's heroic deed, compared to the death, that Jesus had endured for us. He has forever altered the direction of our spiritual journey. His death continues to have the most profound significance on our lives and deaths, as His Son's demise has the ability to alleviate all people from their sins, including people from the past (B.C.), present, and future. Let us not forget, that we must request His Son's cleansing forgiveness, before He agrees to shower us with His pardons. I humbly believe, that we should confess our sins to our Higher Power and His Son daily, since each of us should be responsible for baring the weight of regret for our iniquities, as we should promise Jesus that we will attempt not to sin again. Our Higher Power's knowledge is absolute, as His insight includes the answers to how, when, and why the culmination of the world will indeed happen one day, however, He has not shared this information with His Son, just yet. He comprehends everything that occurs, as He is an energy which remains around and through each of us, at all times. Also, Our Higher Power knows each of our hearts so well, that He remains capable of discerning how we will act and react towards various matters we encounter. Every one of us, continues to carve out his own pathway on earth, since He offers us the freedom to do so. His Son will then receive our soul and its naiveté into an afterlife. I humbly believe that our Higher Power will also welcome us all, as we will one day be united in Heaven with our brothers and sisters of other religions, however, when our brothers and sisters are gently swept-up into the arms of Jesus, they will immediately know Christianity such as Christians do. There are no diversified religions in Heaven. What an unimaginable offering of overflowing, unconditional love, that our Higher Power has bestowed upon us. Ultimately, we are here, due to His immense love and compassion, as He gave us His only Son, who we put to death, even though His Son continues to forgive all of our sins. There must always be a death, in order to create an opening for someone else to live; and therefore, in this circumstance, our souls are the beneficiaries of His Son's death, as His death was destined to occur.

Chapter 4: Our Afterlife

Let us not be ruled by our sinful passions, which cause evil and corruption to fester. Instead of provoking the prince of darkness, let us pay close attention to Jesus, as His earthly life is about to expire, while He lay stretched-out over His cross. Due to the death He executed for the good of our souls, He has been able to grant us an exceptional afterlife; one of which will gloriously exist for eternity, where we shall be in communion with the Entities of the Complete Being. Even though Jesus physically endured an excruciating death, He was also in agony due to the transgressions we had performed, as many of us had become closer to the prince of darkness, while having sailed farther away from Jesus, and His Father. Subsequent to our deaths, when He shall gently place His merciful hands around each of our souls in order to delicately cradle them and carry them into either the temporary premises or Heaven, we will genuinely feel the intensity, and understand the unconditional part of His everlasting love, for the very first time. Through His death, He gives us life, as we are now able to begin our eternal journey. His forgiveness of our transgressions is at the core of why He had to die for our souls. We should never allow the prince of darkness to pressure his destructive ways upon our sensibilities, since he will gladly help us skew our belief system towards his ignorance, as this action will cause us to back away from our Higher Power, which will result in a type of death, in which our Higher Power shall be absent from us in our afterlife, for a longer period of time in the temporary premises, than is necessary. The temporary premises is similar to a waiting room for all tainted souls, which shall eventually enter God's Heaven. As it is written in the Book of Wisdom, "Court not death by your erring way of life, nor draw to yourselves destruction by the works of your hands. Because God did not make death, nor does he rejoice in the destruction of the living." Also stated in the Book of Wisdom, as it is written, "For if the just one be the son of God, he will defend him and deliver him from the hand of his foes." This quote illuminates the wicked individuals, who happened to mock and entice our Higher Power with these blasphemous words. These words were false, simply because He did not "defend," nor "deliver His Son from the hand of his foes," since this was not our Higher Power's desire at that moment in time. God had to make sure that Jesus indeed fulfilled the promise of His death, as He became our Savior, and therefore, God refused to deliver Him from His captors, as our souls were uppermost in our Higher Power's 'mind.' The souls of the individuals which were called into their afterlife by our Higher Power, prior to His Son's appearance on earth, were gathered, protected, and judged by our Higher Power's Law, as God placed and kept these souls in a form of an afterlife. I call this afterlife, the transitory afterlife, which is currently a mystery to us, however, we know that it is an area which kept people's souls, from the time of Adam's death, through the time B.C., Before Christ. The souls, which exist in God's transitory afterlife, were awakened upon His Ascension, and transported by our Savior, to an area called the temporary premises. I imagine that the transitory afterlife, could be likened to a quasi-like state of suspended animation, where there happened to be no suffering, since these souls could not recognize the absence of God's company. All souls complete their travel into the afterlife, by entering the temporary premises. Jesus, immediately after His Ascension, now remains in Heaven for the purposes of fulfilling the Complete Being, and determining the judgment of our souls. Jesus will adjudicate, and then cleanse all of our souls within this temporary premises, after we request His absolution. There were very few souls which were instantly brought into God's Heaven, since almost all, with few exceptions, were sinners. Some of us may view the temporary premises as a kind of purgatory, however, it is not really comparable to this concept, since our souls shall not be placed within an area where we must suffer. His Son shall pardon those, who should be pardoned, and those who are not pardoned on their first pass, will spend more time within the temporary premises, as this becomes our hell, since we are held against our will, as we have a profound need to be with our Higher Power and the Entities. We may be repressed from entering Heaven for a very, very long time, as this depends upon the iniquities which we possess within our soul, and unfortunately, we had not asked Jesus to absolve us of these sins, while we were on earth. He, therefore, continues to give us a negative answer to our dire need, which contains a strong desire to be gently swept-up into Heaven. Hell, as in fire and brimstone, does not exist for us. I also believe that not one of our souls was meant to enter into the everlasting fire. The prince of darkness still remains in hell; however, our souls will never clamor to leave this horrific afterlife. This representation of hell, with our souls buried in a fire pit with the prince of darkness torturing us, does not exist. Our true hell occurs when we must remain in the temporary premises for a longer period of time than usual, since our need is to be with our Higher Power and that necessity is kept from us. Let us all bow to our Savior, and realize that we would not have been transferred into Heaven from the temporary premises, or from the transitory afterlife, without our Savior's death, and without His Father's unconditional love. Jesus died so that our souls could live; and live means existing within a most beautiful of lives, with our Higher Power. All souls, which were gently embraced, and continue to be gently embraced by Jesus, prior to our eternal reward in Heaven, are adjudicated by the expansion and strength of the faith we sustained within our soul on earth. As it is written, "For we hold that a man is justified by faith apart from observance of the law. Does God belong to the Jews alone? Is he not also the God of the Gentiles? Yes, of the Gentiles too. It is the same God who justifies the circumcised and the uncircumcised on the basis of faith." Some of the Books in the Old Testament foreshadow the coming of Jesus. When God appears and the Christian revelation begins within the Old Testament, information regarding God and His Son starts to unfold, while our enlightenment fulfills us more, with each subsequent quote. As it is written, "For God formed man to be imperishable...;" and secondly, "But the souls of the just are in the hands of God, and no torment shall touch them;" and thirdly, "Thus says the Lord: Observe what is right, do what is just; for my salvation is about to come, my justice, about to be revealed," and lastly, "Therefore I will give him his portion among the great, and he shall divide the spoils with the mighty, Because he surrendered himself to death and was counted among the wicked; And he shall take away the sins of many, and win pardon for their offenses." "Whatever you declare bound on earth shall be bound in heaven; and whatever you declare loosed on earth shall be loosed in heaven." See Chapter 30 for an explanation of this quote. His Son speaks to each one of us in this quote, as each one of us lives in a reality of our own construction. We also come from various circumstances and situations, which shall be measured by the imprint left on our souls, as these imprints come from our failed trials on earth. Even though we all emerge from 'different worlds,' the basic logic of what is good and what is bad, should be closely understood by all; no matter which religion we follow. Our Higher Power exhibits some anger within the Old Testament, which He does not exhibit within the New Testament. I humbly believe, that this wonderfully stark difference within our Higher Power's mood towards us, gloriously arrives when Jesus is born, as our Higher Power no longer must punish our sinful deeds, nor must our souls be sent to the transitory afterlife, since Jesus, who made His Father content, now has the capability of absolving our transgressions, subsequent to His Ascension. I find Jesus to be a kinder and a gentler God, whose mercy will never be unabated, although I firmly believe that our Higher Power loves us exactly the same in both Testaments, as He will always love us unconditionally. Each Testament is told as a story unto its own; however, there is a thread which runs across and binds the Old Testament to the New Testament, as we start to understand that the entire Living Scripture, is a pure and a faith-based spiritual biography; a story of humanity and of the Divine. I believe, we fully recognize that the two halves of the Bible make perfect sense together, as they have become complete within, and dependent upon each other.

Chapter 5: Bible Study

Attending an enlightening Bible study is a wonderful place to appreciate the astounding journey of life we have been granted. As we return to Bible study each week, we begin to form an intellectual key, which eventually unlocks the spiritual doors that have bits of important information inside of them. When we start to gather these pieces of information like pieces of a puzzle, we build an understanding of the Scripture at these substantive classes. Being that we are His children, let us begin to contemplate upon what He spiritually desires for us, and act upon His wishes accordingly. One day, I happened to be on campus at the Performing Arts Center, where I was attending college. I desperately needed a peaceful place to complete my homework, so I climbed a set of stairs, where I knew there happened to be a quiet alcove at the summit. When I arrived at the alcove, it was full of young men and young women sitting in a circle. Each of them held a book opened on their laps, as they fervently discussed the content of their book. I could not correctly assess the name of this book, until the leader of the group warmly welcomed me to his Bible study. I quickly sat down, as another person was kind enough to share her Bible with me, for the remainder of the study. The leader mentioned a certain verse aloud, and everyone quietly landed on what seemed to be the very same page, as I could tell by the thickness that existed on each side of their Bibles. Later that very day, I called home and requested a Bible of my own. I guess I had not thought of simply purchasing one at the campus bookstore. Since I am curious, I had the desire to study and readily comprehend the Scripture for myself, however, I did not know where to begin reading to accomplish this task. Therefore, I started at the very beginning, however, my attempt at reading Genesis did not last for very long. I became overwhelmed by the language rather quickly. It was as if the wording and phraseology of the Bible, happened to exist as a unique and eloquent language; one of which I could not fully comprehend, as it appeared somewhat foreign to me.

Every Sunday, at mass, three passages from the Bible are read to us from the pulpit, however, this is different, since we do not have to understand the passages directly from the Bible, as they are dissected and spoon-fed to us by a clergy member. You may never have been part of a Bible study before, however, it is a good way to begin to learn and discern some of the key passages in your Bible. When you are alone, you should attempt to dissect some of the smaller passages, which will give you some confidence in reading your Bible more often. You may choose to execute a passage by memorizing the words, however, listen closely to the intent of these words. You may wish to compare what the words signify, to what the entire passage means. This helped me to start inching my way towards understanding a few of the passages. I found that I was able to speak with our Higher Power regarding the Biblical information I had read, as this conversation was on a deeper level than I had ever encountered. Our Higher Power was sending me a sign that I should remain in this Bible group, since I was indeed ripe for this entire and complex experience. After a week passed, I entered the class once again, as the leader read a verse aloud. All of a sudden, I heard my name called to offer an opinion as to what a particular verse signified. The interpretation I gave was utterly incorrect, but the leader refused to give up on me, as he gave me a supplementary passage to attempt. At this point, even though I felt demoralized, the leader was so very kind and gentle, since he willingly assisted my interpretation of the supplementary passage; I was so relieved. As I started to improve, I discovered that there may be differing interpretations of our Scripture. In my humble opinion, the true art of reading the Bible consists of reading and re-reading the same verse, as we must pray to our Higher Power for the insight we need, to understand the accurate expression of the Scripture. I call my Bible a living Entity, since my interpretation of these familiar passages may change ever-so-slightly, or possibly dramatically, depending on my travels and on the variety of experiences I have encountered. We also listen and learn from others, such as from our clergy members, and from our spiritually, well-informed friends, who continue to join various Bible studies. As I continue to proceed on my own, I begin to underline the passages inside of the New

Testament, which speak to my soul. These are the first passages I find necessary to re-read, if circumstances in my life are going awry, and I am not currently pursuing the pathway to His Truth. If I had not climbed those stairs in the Performing Arts Center as a freshman, my life may have taken quite a different path; one of which would not have been so spiritually enriching. I, however, know in my heart, that I would have eventually looked into attending a Bible study, due to my curiosity, and the immense love and respect I have for our Lord.

Chapter 6: To the Least of My Brothers

"I assure you, as often you did it for one of my least brothers, you did it for me," as it is written. In other words, selfless acts such as: simply listening to others, teaching the illiterate to read, giving hope to a friend in a nursing home, or donating a warm coat to someone in need, ultimately signifies that we are sympathetic to the primal voices of others. We choose to behave in such a solicitous manner, since our Higher Power, who lives within each of our souls, specifically designed us in a way in which we have the desire to help arrest one another's discomfort and misery. Our Creator, who loves nothing more than His children, would not approve of us, if we did not maintain a certain degree of concern, or care for His ultimate creation. Many times, we are frightened of just being too geographically close to the "least of my brothers," as we are taught not to interact with the homeless, or with the poor, who harmlessly ask us for a few dollars in order to eat. When we listen to the morning news regarding how several people in our city have been attacked, we should understand that some of these injured people are the mentally ill, as they are easy targets for individuals, who have a malicious intent. I am suggesting that if there is a way for us to donate a few dollars, or a necessary piece of clothing to the indigent, then we should do so, even if we are faced with this privilege by giving directly to the person, instead of donating through a non-profit first. Even though, a number of people who live on our streets are mentally ill, the majority of them are non-confrontational, however, they desperately require our assistance. This is essential for all of us, and since time is limited, we must adjust the policies of tomorrow into the actions of today. The students, who are now graduating with a psychology or sociology degree from a college or university, and happen to secure a job with the government, should reflect upon how they might best mend the problems of the homeless and mentally ill. We need individuals with fresh eyes and solid training, to look deeply into these unfortunate situations, so that some unique strategies will eventually come forth. I understand that some psychologists and sociologists have been working in order to solve these queries, however, these intelligent people do not seem to want to share their resources, nor function together, in order to resolve these unwanted conundrums. As we help others who are in need, we also indirectly assist ourselves, since we feel the tranquility and satisfaction concerning our interactions with our brothers and sisters, who happen to be homeless. We feel a special warmth and contentment within our hearts, when we connect with another human being on the most basic of levels, as we are willing to feed someone and give them food for the body and food for the soul; we offer them what they truly need. Let us be considerate and nurturing when relating to the indigent and the mentally ill. It is not necessary to see His Son in the flesh in order to have faith in Him. We know that He is with us, since we can observe His sweet Spirit, in the good works all of us execute. These good works please Him, since He appreciates the generosity we gladly share with others. The Entities of the Complete Being are at peace, when we care for each other. We pray directly to our Creator, since He also lives within the souls of "the least of my brothers." All of us should understand that each of us belongs to a sector of "the least of my brothers."

Chapter 7: Children of God/ Karma

"Let the children come to me. Do not hinder them. The kingdom belongs to such as these," as it is written. Little children come alive with a certain innocence and excitement, when they begin to learn about our Higher Power, the angels, and Heaven. The little children listen to this wondrous description, as some of them feel as if Heaven sounds like a beautiful, and a magical place. Even though they wonder what Heaven looks like, the little children refuse to doubt the immense love our Higher Power has for them. Little children exhibit an uncomplicated love for our Father. This love is pure and filled with promises of being good little boys and good little girls, since they know that this pleases Him. They also learn that our Higher Power despises all types of sin, and therefore, most children attempt to fulfill His will. The little children do not cloak Him in misrepresentations and falsifications, which some adults happen to do, since these adults tend to search for answers to difficult spiritual questions, by unknowingly attributing false characteristics to Him. As adults, we tend to assign various qualities to our Higher Power, so that we may try to understand Him better in order to love Him more, however, the little children simply love Him because He exists. As it is written, "Blest are the single hearted for they shall see God." Our Higher Power desires that all of us accept Him with abiding faith and without question. I believe that those adults who live their faith, just as the little children do, shall be wonderfully blessed in the next life, since their strong faith, coupled with their simplistic, unadorned love, will not be questioned. We as adults, will always remain His children, however, we tend to question His behaviors and motives, which is unlike the queries of His little children, as their only communication with our Higher Power remains their loving prayers. We, as His children, are not meant to be perfect, and therefore, let us follow the example of the little children, who see nothing less than His perfect love. As we revel in this thought, we feel relaxed and delighted in the everlasting love He bestows upon us; not for any one reason, however, just because His love is unconditional and endless. Who is our Higher Power? He is a profound Entity for whom we are most grateful, as we receive an impression of His palpable emotions, which we fully experience as a warm and energetic love, as He will give this gift to us continuously, if we fully let Him enter our souls and our lives. We do not simply love our Higher Power due to the fact that He loves us unconditionally, however, we also choose to love Him, since He helps us when we are most desperate for His aid, as we can call upon Him at any time. He is a shining example to all of His children, since He assists each of us; even during the times we choose not to communicate with Him. We should consider this a true lesson in solicitude and love. When His children take care of each other, then He is most pleased. Even though He does at times become disenchanted with a number of our life choices, His unabated love and concern for us does not fluctuate. All He desires is our unwavering devotion, and our enduring love, since we will always be His children, forevermore. Why does our Higher Power allow so much pain in our lives, if He loves His children unconditionally? Our Higher Power grants us the freedom we need, to ultimately make our own decisions concerning our own lives. It is in these active decisions that bring about certain consequences, which we may or may not desire. The cosmos, through our Higher Power, usually only sends forth the karma that we deserve, according to the actions we perform. I believe that karma's repercussive effect, as we get back what we have given, is a pure result of the rebound energy derived through God's 'fingertips.' This energy was given to the cosmos early on, as the cosmos is responsible for setting-up, and doling out either a reward or a punishment, dependent upon our actions. All positives and negatives must add up to zero, when the world ends. Karma is either a reward for an action we performed, or a punishment for an action we should not have executed. If we conduct ourselves favorably, the consequence of our actions should provide us with good karma, which is a positive outgrowth from our behavior. Good or bad karma does not usually deliver a large impact, however, sometimes it may. For instance: good karma could be comprised of finding the last parking spot at the movies, and bad karma could be comprised of tripping and falling over a rock. At times, even though we perform in a responsible manner, we still may experience some bad karma. It seems to be random; however, karma is not randomly dispensed. This scenario has happened to all of us; but why? The explanation is a simple one, in that we have not yet obtained the karma from a prior bad act, in which we were originally involved, as karma is not always given to us in a perfectly time-dependent manner. Let us compare karma to the game of pool. All of us represent the balls within the triangle. Even though the pool cue represents Adam, this pool cue remains in Eve's control. The snake, or the prince of darkness is represented by the cue ball, as he manipulates and tempts Eve into taking the first shot, which ultimately determines that the snake will have some type of influence over all of us, as the cue ball originally makes contact with some of the balls, and those balls make contact with the remainder of the other balls. This is significant, since we will have either been directly, or indirectly touched by the cue ball. The three of them: Adam, Eve, and the prince of darkness, set the specific sinful tone for all of humanity, by sending the balls into their journey forevermore. They helped to drive karma into its progression, as Adam and Eve both ate the forbidden fruit, which was due to the manipulative coaxing given to them by the prince of darkness. The basis for the pool analogy is that, it shows us how karma began and still functions to this very day. In this example, karma was given back to Adam and Eve, in a timely manner, as both of them received some bad karma rather quickly, as a result of the major blunder they executed. Both of them, in addition to all of the generations forthcoming, shall be responsible for their error in judgment, as this outcome will be forever bathed in bad karma; for God's Word and actions are clearly documented in Genesis.

Chapter 8: Our Internal Dialogue

Our internal dialogue is critical to our well-being, since our minds utilize it to construct our morale. It also regulates how we interact and function within our world. We listen to what others reveal to us through a filter, which can either be positive or negative, depending on our moods and/or our beliefs at the moment. This filter contains a loop without an opening, as information is passed directly unto itself multitudes of times, which ultimately leads to our morale, without our knowledge. We have the ability to learn how to alter our morale in a more positive direction, by directly informing ourselves concerning what made our morale so low. For instance, I have a friend, who experienced the end results of having some liposuction on her stomach. I thought she looked great, and I was aware that she had received some wonderful compliments on her new appearance; however, she could not grasp the affirmation given to her by others, because when she gazed at herself in the mirror, she did not notice the great job that her surgeon had performed. She stated, that her stomach looked as though she had not had any liposuction, by the way she appeared in her mirror. I believe this is called, body dysmorphia. My friend allowed her brain to hop onto a loop of destruction, which was internally achieved without her knowledge. As it is written, "Finally, draw your strength from the Lord and his mighty power. Put on the armor of God, so that you may be able to stand firm against the tactics of the devil." We should inquire about reinforcements from our Higher Power, which could function against the dark force, and assist our positive filter to be more involved with our inner emotions. Imagine how hurtful and distracted we would feel, if we only focused on what our negative filter said to us? At certain times, our negative filter is associated with the prince of darkness, as he never seems to relinquish the mighty struggle, which occurs within ourselves. I believe that the dark force undermined her morale, as her consciousness created an incessant, unhealthy loop, which demoralized her. Reflecting upon the abuse of this negative internal dialogue in her mind, we find that it is of the utmost importance to terminate this destructive loop, so that she may not acquire degenerative mental changes, later on in life. I believe that we should try as diligently as we can, to look at various situations through our positive filter. We are all cognizant of the mind-body connection, and therefore, if we use our positive filter more often, our consciousness will help us to feel some relief and contentment. If we have a contradictory or a stubborn personality, the situation at hand will automatically, most likely be translated through our negative filter. Let us try to see the positive and the good in ourselves more often. This is when I attempt to look at each circumstance with decided affirmation, and therefore, focus on my internal dialogue, as it becomes healthy and makes me content. I understand that everything cannot be seen through our positive filter, however, we can make a concerted effort to use our positive filter more often. All of this thinking occurs within a very short span of time, due to the wonderful complexity of our brain, which manipulates many matters at one time. If it is a choice of either retaining a positive or a negative filter at a certain moment, it is our understanding of various circumstances, or our mood, which generally controls this choice of which filter we shall use. Even though our internal dialogue can ultimately be illogical or impractical, we do possess the skill set in order to temper these unsettling thoughts, as they enter our minds. If there are disturbing words spoken to us, our minds are strong enough to declare, 'cancel, cancel, this is untrue, and I refuse to accept this about myself.' Let us be vigilant in our attention to negative filters and destructive loops, simply since they are harmful, as well as magnifying these unnecessary depressive moods in all of us. Our Higher Power trusts that we shall be appeased concerning our intrinsic communication, therefore, let us be free from the malevolent thoughts about ourselves, so that we may concentrate on more spiritually significant matters.

Chapter 9: Love Your Neighbor

As it is written, "...You shall love your neighbor as yourself," which happens to be one of my favorite quotes. Our Higher Power presents us with this comforting declaration, which signifies that the love and consideration we give to ourselves, shall equally be bestowed upon others; as our love shall be granted to others, with just as much honesty and fervor, as we have given to ourselves. Love translates into each of our realities as: kindness, tenderness, and solicitousness. We use the word love, as its many meanings bloom into good intentions, however, we must have enough patience to utilize these intentions, as they must eventually become a benefit to others. The people who we sincerely show concern and compassion for, should not only include the people we know and like. Our love, however, should include all of the people we meet during our lives, as we are all neighbors in the eyes of God. Our Higher Power also asks of us, to love and show mercy towards our enemies. I understand that this will be a difficult process to practice; however, we shall attempt to ethically satisfy this request, in order to fulfill His will. Many factors, such as issues with communication between the two parties, may become troublesome, as we may offend the other party, with or without the benefit of our awareness. If I become aware of any hostility or frustration exuding from my neighbor, which is meant for me, allow me not to become petty nor spiteful. Even though I hear a few choice words forwarded my way, allow me to remain selfless, so that I will not answer another individual, with some of my own mean-spirited language. A good example of a neighbor's love took place between myself and a tow-truck operator. My car had broken down on the highway last year, and I had to call for a tow-truck operator, to relieve my frenzy and confusion. I spoke with him on my phone, and he was supposed to tow me to his garage within fifteen minutes of my call. I saw fifteen minutes tick by; then thirty minutes; and finally, after waiting two hours, with no way to get home, the tow-truck operator finally appeared and apologized. Unfortunately, I was already livid, due to the excessive amount of time it took for him to arrive on scene. I barked a few hurtful words towards him, about his mediocre attempt in securing my car, as he left me struggling on the side of the road, alone, much too long. Thankfully, he rescued me, and my car was eventually fixed the following day. As I went back to the garage to pick up my car, I overheard a few people conversing about an accident, which had occurred just about three miles from where my car had broken down, yesterday. As I joined the conversation, I discovered that the tow-truck operator, who had responded to my call, had to instead go to this accident, where he desperately worked on extricating a woman from her car, during the time he was supposed to be helping me. This remained the reason why he was so late for my call. The person whom they were trying to free, ultimately lost her life on scene due to a crushed trachea. I listened with remorse in my soul; first for the woman who lost her life, and then for those ugly words I had declared towards the tow-truck operator. How I wish I could have recanted those offensive words. He seemed to understand my anxiety, and my expectation that his service would be timely. Since his timeliness was not delivered, he had allowed me the space to express myself without his temperament being disturbed. I admired that about him. Therefore, if we are in the position to assist our neighbor, we should fill our minds with a calm disposition. Let us simply continue to serve our neighbor in need, while we look for the virtue in others and put their imperfections aside; just as he had done with me. Let us also exhibit our internal light, which shines through our eyes and our innocent smile, as this illumination is our Higher Power, who gleams from our soul, when we attend to our neighbors with a most merciful love. We are an integral part of something remarkably unique. Our Higher Power has created each of our souls in an exceptional way, as we are born from Him and eventually continue onto an afterlife of holiness and glory. However, since we still remain on this earth for now, let us use our patience and forgiveness with which The Holy Spirit has endowed us, as we learn to treat each other with mercy and love.

Chapter 10: Challenges

As it is written, "...He will not let you be tested beyond your strength. Along with the test, he will give you a way out of it so that you may be able to endure it." In other words, our Higher Power will not allow us to face a challenge, which will supersede our capability in finding a proper solution. If we do not have the ability to solve a challenge at first, He has promised to provide us with other avenues, which will lead us to the solution. Let us acknowledge and appreciate The Holy Spirit, who has created the ingenuity we need, to effectively temper a difficult situation. As life sends us crises and troubles from which we would like to surrender, His Sacred Words remind us that we will invariably succeed, if we simply continue to sustain the faith in our Higher Power. Let us believe in the words He promised us, since He took a vow, which will provide us with the means to overcome these numerous challenges. Every day, people are asked to achieve what seems to be an impossibility. I am aware of such a case. My friend once knew a woman, who sadly had just buried her spouse due to stage 4 metastatic cancer. She was placed in a difficult dilemma, since she had to care for her three children, alone. She was about forty years of age; however, she had only worked as a waitress. This gave her just enough money to buy food for herself, and her family. The money her and her husband had accumulated in their bank account, which was meant for their retirement, had to be utilized for other important matters, such as her rent and healthcare insurance. Her sixteen-year-old son managed to sense her financial plight, and decided to secure a job at a gas station, during the weekends. He was able to assist his mother by defraying the cost of the monthly rent and food bills. Therefore, let us look closely at all prospects, which might help us to possibly overcome our most arduous challenges. Perseverance will deliver us, as our Higher Power will help us to manage our dilemmas with His guidance and support. We shall eventually tame and conquer our challenges, under His auspices.

Chapter 11: Chronic Illness/Dark Force

Some of us are afflicted with a chronic illness, whether it be mental or physical in nature. When we acquire or are born with such a chronic illness, it is simply due to our bad fortune. The possibility of reaping such an illness, is not the fault of bad karma, since this is much too severe a punishment for which karma should normally be responsible. The scenario of this child's birth took place when karma first smiled upon the meeting of two strangers, who happened to become proud parents; however, their DNA unfortunately rendered their child infirm, the moment he was born with a chronic illness. Just as Jesus was teased and taunted by the prince of darkness on the mountain, our Higher Power also permits us to be tormented through our illness. As it is written, "Do not be surprised, beloved, that a trial by fire is occurring in your midst. It is a test for you, but it should not catch you off guard. Rejoice instead, in the measure that you share Christ's sufferings. When his glory is revealed, you will rejoice exultantly. Happy are you when you are insulted for the sake of Christ, for then God's Spirit in its glory has come to rest on you." Even though the torment we endure through the dark force is arduous, we will defeat him in the end. This evil and vile force takes advantage of us through our sickness, by increasing our symptomatology, and our pain. The result of this increase in pain, nudges us towards the direction of our Higher Power, as we begin to implore Him for the solace, and the peace that we need. Since we have a chronic illness, we should begin to utilize this platform as a starting point of discourse and prayer, if we do not already have a running dialogue with Him. We should wish to invariably keep in close contact with our Higher Power. Let us never allow ourselves to follow the dark force's temptations and worldly ways; just as we should never bow down to the prince of darkness, even if he promises us certain relief from our illness. The prince of darkness is alive and well, as he causes hatred and evil to enter our lives. When we become too engrossed in the matters of this world, we should awaken quickly, since he coerces our minds to depart with him amid his immoral existence, thereby causing us to distance ourselves from our Higher Power. The prince of darkness can wrap vicious propositions and circumstances, with shiny wrapping paper and pretty bows, as these bows sit perched atop lovely wrapped packages, so that we become enticed and monopolized by them. For instance, I have a good friend, who has a gambling addiction, and he unfortunately cannot free himself from this nasty habit. The shiny wrapping paper, in this example, functions as his hope; as he continuously hopes to win a million dollars, by playing black jack at the casino. The dark force speaks loudly into his ears, so that he becomes distracted and deafened, as he cannot thoughtfully consider the detriment which happens day after day, as he continues to lose his hard-earned money, and his family. As it is written, "When an unclean spirit has gone out of a man, it wanders through arid wastes searching for a resting-place; failure to find one, it says, 'I will go back to where I came from. It then returns, to find the house swept and tidied. Next it goes out and returns with seven other spirits, far worse than itself, who enter and dwell there. The result is that the last state of the man is worse than the first." He tried to tame his gambling addiction more than once, however, this seems to be impossible, since he genuinely has not been able to suspend his efforts while betting, or taking a risk, for more than a few hours at a time. The dark force remains in control of this man, which is what the prince of darkness desires, since he wishes to 'chip away' at the goodness of our Higher Power. People who worship the excitement of winning, tend to completely discount their faith and hope in our Higher Power, as they begin to throw all of their spiritual connections and family bonds aside. Similarly, addiction to narcotics, or opioids, may alleviate our misery when we have migraine headaches or back pain, however, these pills begin to be overly utilized, and our time with our Higher Power starts to decrease, as the misuse of our narcotic painkillers begins to increase. If we are under the influence of a mind-altering drug, we might never notice when our sacred relationship with Him begins to slip away, until it has disappeared. We would not have the ability to speak with our Higher Power in a genuine manner, nor with the sincerity of a cleansed mind and soul. At times, it is necessary for some of us to suffer from migraine pain, or from other types of pain, since it will heighten our desire to initiate, and to nourish a strong bond between us and God, as we will call upon Him to relieve us from our pain, and ultimately, spend more time praying to Him. As the amount of medication we consume begins to decrease, we should sincerely thank Him for His assistance when our pain begins to subside. Since prayer leads us closer to our Higher Power, we may consequently lean on Him, in lieu of living without our supplementary medication. The reduction of medication will enable us to comprehend Him in a more substantial, and in a more profound way. As we graduate, from strictly conversing with Him regarding our pain control, we begin to ascertain that we can pray to Him, for all of our other troubling matters. We may also desire to appreciate certain circumstances, with which He has gifted us, as we may ultimately wish to share our appreciation of Him, because He is our God.

Chapter 12: Absolution

Each time we confess our sins to His Son, He relieves our troubled souls. As we begin to pray to Him for our deliverance, our unsettling transgressions will be absolved. The response to our petitions should not be as important, as being capable of continuing our communication with His Son, whether we are moved to do so or not. Just because He does not answer our prayers immediately, does not mean that He is too engrossed in other matters to respond to us. He who knows all answers to all questions understands better than we do. Therefore, it may not be wise to deliver us from our transgressions, and help us to change, quite so swiftly. Perhaps the reason for the delay is that we have not yet repented enough in our hearts. Perhaps, He may derive enjoyment from the additional conversational prayers, we offer Him; or perhaps the delay lies within the following Scripture passage, "...I will show mercy to whomever I choose; I will have pity on whomever I wish. So, it is not a question of man's willing or doing, but of God's mercy," as it is written. This passage describes His mercy and His leniency, as He will give each of us His compassionate gift of absolution, and will endow each of us with His wondrous gift of Heaven, to whomever He chooses; as all other questions regarding this subject matter are of no importance. Our absolution, and our entrance into Heaven are not circumstances that can be worked on, or remain hopeful for, but they are circumstances that will only occur through the generosity of His mercy. We must ask Him for forgiveness, in order to receive His mercy and therefore, His absolution. We should feel the angst for each sin we execute, for our sins are the reason why our Savior had to enter into His death. Personally, I do not believe that when we enter into an afterlife, we must be sinless. However, I do believe that we must be sinless, when we make our final preparations to enter into Heaven. The Scripture does affirm that His Son's mercy is most important, as each of us departs for an afterlife. His mercy, which is ultimately necessary to enter into Heaven, is not the missing piece of the puzzle; it is indeed, the whole puzzle, as His mercy is all we need, when the power of our faith is being adjudicated. We may have performed as many deeds as we could have, for our neighbors, however, if we perform these deeds without love in our heart, or faith within our soul, then He understands that this ruse is similar to the prince of darkness leading a parched individual to an empty waterhole. Let us remain watchful, so that indifference does not occur, after He has comforted us with the absolution to our iniquities. Indifference, which is not necessarily meant to offend our Father nor His Son, takes place when we carelessly discontinue our prayers, as we turn off our communication with Him, for the desires of this world. Our Higher Power wishes that we would pray to Him daily, however, we are not obliged to pray, due to our free will, even though we should yearn for the same intentions, that our Father wishes for, which is where the conclusion of our souls shall end. I believe that we are extremely fortunate, if we hold onto the intentions of our Higher Power in our thoughts, and we continuously appreciate our primal need for His Son. Let us comprehend and respect the gifts of prayer and faith, and let us continue to converse with Him on a more profound, and a more sustained level.

Chapter 13: A Certain Sadness/Fear

All of us are pestered by a certain sadness, which rears its ugly head every now and again, so that we genuinely feel and act disgruntled. Some of us do not possess the insight to what truly may be bothering us. Therefore, we are compelled to spend time with a counselor or a physician for these answers. Even though we are satisfied, to a certain extent, with the spiritual lives we lead, we still have these tedious melancholic periods which are difficult to navigate. Without bringing this sorrow into our full consciousness, this certain sadness will remain with us. As we reflect upon what this depressed mood may encompass, we start to innately comprehend, that our flesh will eventually cease to exist. This feeling is painful to the core of our brain, as our neurons are responsible for translating neurotransmitters into feelings. Feeling depressed is different than hurting us to the core of our being, since our soul truly wishes to be with our Higher Power, as our soul has already started its journey in Heaven. Our soul shall never die, as it ethereally exists within us; however, our processing center, or the structural components of our brain, do not celestially exist within us, since they are part of the flesh, and will die with the flesh. Therefore, I humbly believe that the certain sadness within us, develops from the portion of our bodies, which can be justified anatomically; not spiritually. As this moment continues to approach, with every tick of the clock, the acute awareness of our demise becomes a catalyst, which contributes to the internal fearfulness of how and when we shall expire. However, we know that the trust we maintain in our Higher Power and His Son, should never be combined with fear. As it is written, "Love has no room for fear; rather, perfect love casts out all fear. And since fear has to do with punishment, love is not yet perfect in one who is afraid." The trust we have acquired, should be strong enough to interrupt this internal, apprehensive feeling. Let us give ourselves completely over to Him, and let us call upon the promises that He made to us. We should become innately overjoyed, as we were promised that we would pass the remainder of eternity with our Creator and our Savior. I believe that The Holy Spirit's gift of faith, helps us to desire an even stronger faith in the Complete Being. We are told to lean upon our faith at all times, and the more we lean, the more powerful our faith will become. As it is written, "I repeat, it is owing to his favor that salvation is yours through faith. This is not your own doing, it is God's gift; neither is it a reward for anything you have accomplished, so let no one pride himself on it." Jesus is the only Being who shall form any decision, concerning which of us shall receive the gift of salvation, as His merciful determination shall be applied, according to the faith we have nourished and sustained. Our journey has already commenced in Heaven, since our souls were originally realized in Heaven, and subsequently, were given by our Higher Power, as our mothers were giving birth to each of us. I humbly believe that our Higher Power, does not choose when each of our souls will enter into His domain. When I communicate with our Higher Power, I am earnest when I inform Him that I am completely ready and at peace to enter His eternal home. The subject of our demise, reminds me of those who have had near death experiences. These specific people claim to have died and understood that the warm, bright Light, which they had traveled towards, belonged to the Entities of the Complete Being, and therefore, none of the people desired to return to the earth alive, as they all wished to remain bathed within this warm, magnificent, white Light. These individuals also stated that they were no longer fearful of death, after they awoke from their incomparable experiences. The accounts they spoke of, certainly piqued my interest. In order to develop internal peace, let us no longer allow our death from the earth to disturb us. If we improve our attitudes and behaviors, we will transition from plain caterpillars, into beautiful butterflies. Subsequent to reflecting upon our trepidation, we should begin to cleanse our internal houses by conversing with His Son regarding our fear. After this cleansing, we hope to live with our newly simple and purified souls, of which there should be no more fear regarding our death, as we have now prepared ourselves for an afterlife full of grace, and full of everlasting love.

Chapter 14: Creationism and Darwinism

Is it possible to reconcile Darwin's Theory of Natural Selection, with the Theory of Creationism? It is important to comprehend exactly how Adam and Eve came into being, and what the field of biology has disclosed to us regarding evolution these many years. First, however, let us primarily recall that the earth is approximately four billion years old, and in my humble opinion, our Higher Power is unquestionably the sole conductor of the incredible explosion, which thrust the vacancy of space aside, thereby creating the origin of the universe. After the creation of the universe, there continues to be less dominate explosions within the void of space, however, these more intimate and elegant explosions, are still powerful enough to give birth to new solar systems and galaxies. When the earth was first formed, there were substances known as primordial clouds, which were suspended above our planet. Darwin gave credit to the primordial clouds, for providing the necessary molecules, which supported life in its delicate infancy. As it rained from the primordial clouds, the dry ocean beds filled with water. The life-giving molecules were then able to fit together perfectly, as the new oceans swirled about, and formed earth's tiniest of animals: the amoebae. Humans have tried to duplicate the environmental condition of the primordial clouds; however, we have not been capable of creating an amoeba, or any other living microscopic animal. Evolution started as soon as the smallest of creatures survived and procreated, as evolutionary transformations still occur in today's world. Creationism defines: how long it took for our Higher Power to create the earth, what occurred on each day, and how long it took to create the first human being. The following three quotes from Scripture will give us a sense of how we have trouble concerning the Complete Being's definition of time, since the time we experience on this planet, does not match our Higher Power's interpretation of time, as He sees and encounters everything during and within the present. As it is written, "For a thousand years in your sight are as yesterday..." also, as it is written, "This point must not be overlooked, dear friends. In the Lord's eyes, one day is as a thousand years and a thousand years are as a day," and lastly, as it is written, "Jesus Christ is the same yesterday, today, and forever." We tried to adapt our frame of reference to His, as our frame of reference includes time, which is segmented into the past, present, and future, however, we continue to attempt how to explain the operation of His world, since it does not branch into the past, nor into the future. The quote which reads, "...a thousand years are as a day," is an oxymoron, however, this inconsistency was written for a reason. I humbly believe that when "a thousand years" was written, it just as well could have been written as a million years. Therefore, when the story of Creationism was expressed to us through Scripture, each of the seven days may have possibly lasted millions, or even hundreds of millions of years. If we multiply hundreds of millions of years, by seven, for the seven days it took for the Creation and the day of rest to occur, we can then arrive at an answer of about four billion years, which is a good approximation to the number of years our planet has been spinning on its axis, within the solar system. Time is simply based on segmented intervals of duration, as Adam and Eve were created around 6,000 B.C. We found that other Homo sapiens, who most resemble modern man from Darwin's evolutionary tree, began living at approximately forty thousand years ago. They did not have the ability to pray, since they were not aware that they did not have a soul, as they were born from a lineage of animals. This genuinely saddened our Higher Power, as He wanted to build a legacy of humans, who listened to His Word, and humans who could communicate with Him. Therefore, a fresh start was essential in order to transcend this conundrum. Our Higher Power decided to mold Adam from the clay of the earth, and to create Eve from Adam, as they were not plucked from the evolution of animals. After God molded Adam with His mighty hands, He gave Adam a soul from Heaven. This process had never happened to any other Homo sapiens, prior to Adam's formation. As it is written, "— the Lord God formed man out of the clay of the ground and blew into his nostrils the breath of life, and so man became a living being." He then created a female partner for Adam, named Eve, as it is written, "This one, at last, is bone of my bones and flesh of my flesh; This one shall be called 'woman,' for out of 'her man' this one has been taken." Eve was also given a soul, as the people who were, and continue to be a part of Adam's lineage are fortunate to be born with a soul. The Homo sapiens, which Darwin classified, had evolved from animals, as they all existed without a soul. They continued to live alongside Adam, Eve, and their progeny, who all lived with a special gift from our Higher Power, since a soul was given to each of them, and currently, to each of us, as we remain descendants of Adam and Eve. As many years passed, both types of Homo sapiens refuse to do what our Higher Power declares, except for a few well-known individuals, who passionately listen to our Higher Power. Noah was one of these individuals who lovingly listened to the Lord, especially when He pronounces that Noah should take-on a special project. When Noah appears in the Bible, God demonstrates His genuine love for him, as He informs Noah, how to build an ark of specific dimension, which will save him and his family from the Great Flood. Noah heeds God's warning, as he and his family do not perish when the rains begin to pour, and the excessive water entombs the earth. All of the Homo sapiens, who evolved from animals, as well as the humans who did not care to listen to, nor love our Higher Power, continued to be inundated with water, as they drowned and were washed away during the Great Flood. After the water had receded, Noah and his family were the only humans that remained alive, as they started a new generation of human beings that were born from his legacy, as all humans would presently continue to be endowed with a soul, which was first created in Heaven. I humbly believe, therefore, that I have been successful in reconciling Darwin's Theory of Natural Selection and the Theory of Creationism. These two Theories overlap for a moment in time, as both types of Homo sapiens lived alongside of each other, until the flood waters washed them all away. We, as His creation remain the only 'Homo sapiens,' or human beings on earth, as there is a distinct difference between Darwin's classification of Homo sapiens, and God's creation of humanity. We must be attentive to what the Holy Scripture declares, and to what it does not, as Scripture must form an entire story, which makes common sense to our intuition, and to our insight.

Chapter 15: Turn the Other Cheek

As it is written, "...When a person strikes you on the right cheek, turn and offer him the other." To genuinely comprehend and process this quote, we need the mind-set of a meek and forgiving person. Initially, I wondered why I should deliver myself, or my will over to an individual who had previously struck me. Should I attempt to escape from such an individual, especially since his intention might be to strike me again? Even though Scripture answers this inquiry negatively, why does our Higher Power declare, that we should grant our abuser another chance to hurt us? Customarily, the person who is hit first, would attempt to subject his abuser to some form of payback. Although this retaliatory maneuver may seem like the right move to make, our Higher Power wants us to humble ourselves, and offer our opponent another chance to strike us, after he has had time to process how it actually feels to hit us. At times, our Higher Power will instruct us through precedents. These are matters which have already occurred, such as the instigator striking us for the first time, as this strike caused a variety of feelings, which the instigator experienced. As we nervously turn to offer him our other cheek, we should remain calm and tolerant of his behavior, since our peaceful demeanor may stimulate the abuser to think twice before striking us again, as our posture demonstrates that we are of no threat to him. Our Higher Power does not wish for the abuser to inflict pain upon us for a second time, however, He desires for us to be a good example during the conflict, and trusts that our opponent may learn civility and benevolence through our action. Even though this is not the popular response, it is the proper and clever reply. We hope that the instigator's combative tendencies will leave him, as he might instead accept a more calming and understanding position. What is significant to our Higher Power, is that through our actions, He can enlighten and guide our abuser, as he learns the self-restraint, which is needed before he possesses an opportunity to strike anyone; next time. As it is written, "Never act out of rivalry or conceit; rather, let all parties think humbly of others as superior to themselves..." If the combative instigator had listened to the thoughts brought forth through this quote, he would have never hit us from the beginning. He would have treated us far better, since he would have never acted from his ego, nor out of rivalry. This entire subject may be extrapolated to form examples, other than that of physical abuse; the same template may be used to emotionally or intellectually be abused by others, or perhaps be the abuser. Let us lay the abuse of others to rest, so that we may find favor with our Higher Power.

Chapter 16: Dying an Exceptional Death

Why did God send His only Son to suffer and die on a wooden cross, instead of coming to fulfill this holy death on planet earth, Himself? There are three main reasons why our Higher Power could not satisfy and complete the act of the crucifixion. First, each Entity within the Complete Being functions with a primary purpose, which the Father had assigned to each of the three: The Father functions as the Creator of life and Delegator of each task; His Son functions as our Savior and Final Judge; and The Holy Spirit functions as our Messenger and grants us our special gifts and talents. Secondly, the Father must oversee all of our souls, and even though He lives everywhere, He primarily resides in Heaven. Thirdly, our Higher Power does not wish for us to see and experience Him in all of His glory just yet, as He chooses to continue to be an enigma to us, while we are on earth. This remains one of the Sacred Mysteries. Each one of the three Entities are responsible for the usage of their own unique attributes, which remain distinctive and non-interchangeable. For instance, His Son is the only Entity who could become our Savior, as it is His Son's duty to listen to His Father's disclosures, and act accordingly. The three Entities also possess some core attributes, which are identical and interchangeable, some of which include: mercy, kindness, and patience. Heaven is the dominion of the Entities of the Complete Being, and therefore, we should not expect to be delivered into the Entities' domain. Heaven is a gift, for which we should be thankful, as this thought allows us to continually acknowledge His boundless generosity, when we communicate with Him through prayer. His Son promises that He will be merciful towards us, if we are able to maintain our faith, compassion, and forgiveness towards others, as He gives us the opportunity to learn from His actions, as well as to learn from the essence of His Words. As we listen intently to our Savior, the reflection of His Words, will eventually trickle into our minds and our souls. Our caring and compassion for others should be worthy of what the Beatitudes declare concerning mercy, which is stated in the Sacred Scripture of Matthew. The ultimate way to demonstrate that you love someone, is to die for that individual, thereby imparting life to that individual in the end. Forgiveness is considered the most significant part of mercy, as His Son is declared the Final Judge, for which all souls will undergo an ultimate adjudication, by the most compassionate, and merciful God. Our faith in the Savior, is derived from the mercy and forgiveness He has exhibited throughout the New Testament. We should continue to cling onto our Savior's vow, that whether we were born prior to, or subsequent to His arrival on earth, each of us, beginning with Adam, shall finally be judged according to the faith we have exhibited throughout our life. As it is written, "For we hold that a man is justified by faith apart from observance of the law." His Son will examine our faith, which is shown through the love we continue to possess for the Entities. Prior to His Son's Ascension, our Higher Power had guided the souls that had already been judged by His Law, into a peace-filled afterlife, as these souls shall be given a chance to repent for their sins in the temporary premises. He pledged, that all of our souls would be saved through His demise. As it is written, "Whoever would save his life will lose it, but whoever loses his life for my sake will find it." The first part of this quote says, "Whoever would save his life will lose it...." This portion explains how we blatantly glorify the riches of this world, since we only seem to care for the items of this world, and place no importance on a relationship with His Son. Therefore, we may possibly lose our souls and His Son's mercy in the end. We say that we love Him, however, we do not spend the time, in prayer, to be with Him. If we love someone, we should want to spend the time to be with them, just as we enjoy spending time with a friend, or a family member. The second part of this quote says, "...whoever loses his life for my sake will find it." This portion declares how we should give up our worldly pursuits, in order to follow His Son, as the word, "loses" signifies a change in our lives, which ultimately leads us to concentrate on a living relationship between us and Jesus Christ. If we "lose" or stop using this world as our playground, we can then focus on a more beautiful life; one that we should start living prior to our demise.

Chapter 17: Sin and Guilt

Let us spend a few special moments with our Higher Power and His Son, as we repent for the sins we perpetrate daily. The process of repentance may be simple enough for us to execute, however, the death He endured for us remains unimaginable. We can sense the weariness in our minds, when we attempt to sympathize with our Savior, during the entire time He carried the cross, and the entire time He was nailed to the cross. We should regret our sinful decisions, since we all share in the burden of being primary participants in the sins we have committed, which is why our Higher Power directed our Savior to come to our planet and die for us, as this one action grants us the extraordinary gift of salvation. Even though we sin daily, the guilt we feel will eventually be washed away, due to His Son's merciful absolution. Each of us is partially to blame, for sending Him to an agonizing death, by thoughtlessly perpetrating one indiscretion at a time. When we ask His Son to pardon us, we can feel our faces suddenly brighten, as our newly disentangled souls are once again free from impurity. Let us remember that His Son's love is unconditional, as He loves us no matter how many transgressions we commit. We should embody the emotion He gives us, as He declares that we should feel utterly valued and worthy, simply due to His love for us. We do not need to hold onto any guilt, due to the sins we committed, since we no longer live for the flesh, nor its satisfaction. The passionate love His Son possesses for us, is phenomenally more profound than we can imagine, therefore, let us not take this extraordinary gift for granted. Let us look forward to our times together in prayer, as we will soon feel His comforting love. We should never use the name of our Lord, as if He were trivial or unimportant to us, although, we know that due to His merciful spirit, we shall always be absolved of this sin, if we ask Him for His forgiveness. As it is written, "Whoever says anything against the Son of Man will be forgiven, but whoever says anything against The Holy Spirit will not be forgiven, either in this age or in the age to come." For instance, declarations against The Holy Spirit involve the following examples; as it is written, "Ananias, why have you let Satan fill your heart so as to make you lie to The Holy Spirit and keep for yourself some of the proceeds from that field?" As it is written, "It is by Beelzebul, the prince of death, that the Spirit of God casts out devils..." This last sentence improperly signifies that The Holy Spirit needs assistance from the prince of darkness, in order to cast the angels of the dark force aside. We know this to be completely false, since The Holy Spirit has the ability to toss these dark angels away from us, even when they occupy the inside of our minds and souls. The Holy Spirit can perform this action on His own, or with the remaining two Entities of the Complete Being; as He does not need the prince of darkness to assist Him with anything. If a human being has: experienced the gifts of The Holy Spirit, listened to the Word of our Higher Power, and then, simply allowed himself to fall away from his beliefs, then this person's thinking must indeed be evil. He has perpetrated a sin, at least in part against The Holy Spirit. I humbly believe that taking the gifts He gave us for granted, is a sin in itself.

Chapter 18: The Mystery of the Complete Being

Why do we find it necessary to pray to our Higher Power, since we are completely aware that He is already cognizant of the exact vocabulary and content, that we are about to disclose in our plea to Him? Let us pray, since prayer strengthens our belief and trust in the knowledge, that there is and will always be a Higher Power. Prayer also strengthens the bond of love held between us, which increases the intensity of our faith, as we are led on a sacred journey, each time we speak with Him. As it is written, "Whenever you pray, go to your room, close your door and pray to Him in private. Then your Father, who sees what no man sees, will repay you." Even though we may be silent at times, since we have unnecessarily discontinued praying for a period of time, we will continue to be supported by our Higher Power in many ways; most of which we are simply not made aware. We can either choose to be alone, or in a group setting, when we prepare to express ourselves to Him. We should realize that the more we communicate with our Higher Power, the better our connection, and the more we shall become willing and satisfied, when we pray. Our love for Him will come naturally, since this will be similar to speaking with a comfortable old friend, day after day. I humbly believe that our Higher Power enjoys listening to factually-based prayers, since they will endow Him with a clear vision of our expressions, and in another sense, they will confirm and affirm what we know to be true. I realize that having a conversation with one of the three Entities, can indeed be a conundrum, when all we hear in the deafening silence, is our thoughts or our whispers. Even though we do not hear His voice with our ears, we do hear Him with our intuition. At times, we feel as if He does not respond to our prayers immediately, however, the cause of the delay may not be a delay at all, since we may not have fully recognized, nor agreed with His reply. Our problem begins when we continue to stare through our tunnel vision, for what we had requested, as we do not look for other possible solutions to our petitions, just yet. Learning to converse with the

Complete Being is perplexing at first, unless we begin to ascertain a mature focus on each individual prayer. Since there is a learning curve for discovering how to manage a conversational prayer with Him, reciting a few rote prayers in order to stimulate our minds, remains a good idea. When we pray, we always seem to mention what we need from Him first, whether this plea is for ourselves, or for others. We usually terminate our conversational prayers with Him at this juncture. Let us, however, think of Him as a friend, a mentor, a father, so that we shall have the ability to speak with Him regarding many other thoughts, such as: what may be troubling us, thanking Him for the blessed circumstances He has given us, and reflecting upon our Scripture readings for the day. I humbly believe that the Sacred Mystery of the three Beings, which exists as one Entity, may be explained in the following way. Let us conceptualize a cool frying pan which is currently holding three uncooked, shelled eggs, which represent the three Entities or Beings; The Father, His Son, and The Holy Spirit. Each Being has an unbroken yoke, and whites which are commixed. These three eggs lay on top of one another, so that when we look at this Entity from above, we shall only see one complete egg, however, we know that there are two other eggs beneath. Each egg white is bonded and interwoven between all three eggs, as each Being shares a portion of Himself with the other two Beings, and a connection is made. However, each Being also remains on His own. This is specified by the unbroken, yet noticeably varied yokes, as our Heavenly Father's yoke is the biggest of the three, even though the Father is not more important than the other two Beings. One Being is not more important than any of the other two, although the Father must remain in the Complete Being for it to function as beautifully and as completely as it does, since He is the authority figure of the Entities, as He delegates the progression of the tasks, which the other two Beings must perform. The Father, Himself, remains cognizant of when, how, and where He must perform His own tasks. One day, one of the Entities prepared to leave the nest of the Complete Being, which occurred when The Father sent His Son down to earth. The three eggs at this time formed into separate whites, so that His Son could travel with His entire unmixed white portion and unbroken yoke to earth, and as a result, He was born all man and all God. The other two whites, within the Complete Being, became commingled once again. There were two unbroken yokes left, just until His Son returned to the other two Beings. As the Son ascended back into Heaven, thirty-three years later, the Complete Being was reformed and restored into a state of perfection. The three eggs, with their white parts commingled, and their varied yokes, have the ability to remain separate, flawless, and different from each other. Of course, the egg scenario was only prepared for this format, in order to explain how one has the ability to form part of three, and three has the ability to form one. As I was writing this scenario, a question came to mind: if the Complete Being has always been here, how could our Higher Power's Son have always been present with His Father, when we know a father to always be older than his son? Perhaps the translation of father and son, is not the best translation to assist our understanding of this mystery. I am familiar with the title, 'God's anointed King,' as 'anointed' here signifies, 'for a special task,' which would more easily accommodate our comprehension of Christ, within the Complete Being, since Christ can be the same age as His Father, if He is perceived as, 'God's anointed King.' The 'special task' refers to the Crucifixion. I just mentioned the phrase, 'the same age,' however, the Entities of the Complete Being are ageless and timeless, since God's world does not encompass or function using time; also, age cannot be determined, since the Entities have always existed. Through our communion with the Complete Being, our conversation remains a blessing, as we are capable of praying for all others; especially those who suffer from various debilitating conditions. As we rightfully pray for these less fortunate individuals, let us be diligent in our request for them, since we know that our prayers can be powerful and beneficial. The people who live with a mental illness, and/or suffer with chronic pain, are dear to my heart, as I converse mostly with our Higher Power concerning these oppressed individuals, who happen to exist all over the world. Therefore, the people who cannot or will not pray for themselves, will receive the benefit from other individuals, who pray for those who cannot pray for themselves, possibly due to depression or other types of psychiatrically-based, or organically-based difficulties. Let us be present with our Higher Power at all times, since we will engage Him, when we focus on holding Him in our thoughts. If a variety of matters in our life proceed improperly, due to our sinful ways, our Higher Power will be with us when we need His wisdom most of all; even if we do not ask for His help. What should we listen for, when He answers our prayers? We may feel a warmth between our chest and abdominal cavities, so that we know that He is undeniably present within us, as I believe that He is directly connecting with our soul, at that particular moment. When He answers our prayers, we will see a change in the person or circumstance, for whom or which we are praying. For example, I happen to pray for someone that I am personally very close to, even though her spirit has always been negative and difficult. She is not content with her own situation or within herself. I pray for her spirit to become light and more joyous, so that she may delight in herself and in our Higher Power. When her spirit does appear more joyful, I know that He also wants her to feel content, as He has answered my prayers. Communication with our Higher Power is unequivocally a blessed event, and each time we acknowledge others in our petitions, we become selfless. Let us pray for others, as Christ gives us the benefit of these petitions and prayers.

Chapter 19: The Essence of Our Soul

Just as an arm or a leg is necessary for helping our bodies perform certain tasks, our soul is even more essential, since it helps us to delineate the right choices for our lives. All human beings are most significantly comprised of a soul, as this gives us the ability to be aware of the special love, we continue to enjoy through our Higher Power. The soul also allows us to comprehend the meaning of what a spiritual life entails; most importantly, our communication with the Entities of the Complete Being. I have been asked if animals have a soul and go to Heaven, and by my definition, they unfortunately do not, since they cannot pray, or have thoughts about a spiritual life, and everything that is associated with this life, such as we can. Animals are not privy to the belief, or to the knowledge that there is a Higher Power. They do, however, have an effervescence or an energy about them, just as all creatures do, and are created from organic molecules, which form all animals, and human beings. I believe that our Higher Power lives as a type of energy; a mystery, which He has not shared with us, just yet. When we pray to Him, we begin to build a reinforced framework for love to prosper, as this love eventually becomes a powerful bond between us. We may feel as though stating our prayer emphatically, or stating our plea multiple times, will help us to receive a response from Him more rapidly. I find that if we state our case well the first time, there is no need for the exact plea to be reiterated, however, this repetition is enough to put my mind at ease, therefore, I do recite my prayer over and again, although, this is not necessary. Praying provides us with a wealth of cognitive support, since when we pray, it greatly helps us to focus our minds on what is important. Furthermore, He knows what the essence of our prayer is, even before we consciously disclose it to Him. At certain times, He may respond to our prayers or pleas, and we do not recognize His answer, since we may be looking for a different reply, than what He has ultimately given us. This remains as a reason, why we should only ask Him for a resolution to our dilemma. Even though it is natural for us to ask for a specific outcome to our problem, we should always include the words: 'let Your will be done,' since this outcome might not necessarily be the result that He desires, nor be the best consequence for everyone involved. We may not fancy what His answer to our prayer happens to be, however, let us remain content with whatever resolution He bestows upon us. "God created man in his image...," as it is written. I humbly believe, that even though we do not assume the appearance, or some semblance of our Higher Power externally, we do, however, resemble Him internally, since His Essence resides within our soul. Deep within us, there is a love which freely flows from our soul. Within the source of this pure and perfect love, we find our soul consists of an Essence, from the 3 Entities and 2 complete spirits. Our soul is composed of: 1. our Higher Power's Essence, 2. Christ's Essence, 3. The Holy Spirit's Essence, 4. our own spirit, which is 'our intrinsic spirit' or our intuitive sense, and 5. our angel of protection, which is a spirit unto its own. Our intuition urges us, and is best utilized when there is a need to determine the right choice over all other choices. There seems to be a specific energy, possibly a type of molecular reconfiguration energy, which allows The Holy Spirit to replicate Himself, or divide Himself, so that He may remain within the Complete Being, while managing all of His responsibilities. Let us live within an illuminated reality, due to the fact that our soul, which was delicately placed within us by our Higher Power, gracefully comes to rest in a particular space in our body, where we can feel Him at any time. My soul rests between my chest and abdominal cavities. "Are you not aware that you are the temple of God, and that the Spirit of God dwells in you?" as it is written. We should be capable of grabbing onto our Higher Power with both hands, and clearly declaring to Him that He is the most important Existence within our lives, as our souls wish to be enlightened and loved by Him, for an eternity.

Chapter 20: Using Various Tools

The Holy Spirit has endowed us with the intelligence and the industriousness to solve many of our own problems. Each of us has been given extraordinary gifts by The Holy Spirit, and therefore, let us not allow these gems to fade, by refusing to utilize the abilities we were given. Allow us to become more proactive regarding our own efforts, when we attempt to solve our numerous daily dilemmas. We may need to look at these conundrums from more than one angle, until they are indeed resolved. Our Higher Power enjoys assisting us as we endeavor to decipher our problems, and attempt to help ourselves. For example, I have a friend who relished the chance to attend his local university, however, he could not join the other students, since he had insufficient funds. He was not permitted to borrow any money from the local bank, due to his poor credit history. His parents also denied him a loan, since they did not have enough capital to lend him. As he saw his options to participate in the freshman class start to dwindle, he happily completed a scholarship form, given to him by the university. In order to acquire this scholarship, he must write an essay on how he would define what the necessities of his community are, and how he would best mend them. After he formulated his essay, he began to pray incessantly, as he started to converse with our Higher Power concerning his desire to obtain this scholarship. He began to pray over and over again, 'Please allow me to secure this scholarship, however, let Your will be done.' Unfortunately, the scholarship was awarded to another student the very next day. Due to his inability to have secured the university scholarship, he spent the next week in a depressed mood, as he became disconcerted and full of self-doubt. However, as he scanned his local paper on Saturday, he quickly read the 'want ads' section, and soon discovered that there was a position open at a local restaurant, for a waiter on the night shift. Subsequent to applying for the waiter's job in person, he received a call-back that night, as he had successfully secured the position. Since he lived rent free with his parents, which was coupled with the money he would receive from his new job, he would then have the ability to sufficiently pay the cost of his entire tuition. He had finally harnessed a useful solution, with our Higher Power's help. Although, this was not the easiest of all solutions, at least it was a solution, which worked for him in the end. Our Higher Power, who never leaves us, promised that He would present us with other avenues, in order to help us resolve our dilemma; not necessarily the way we wanted our dilemma to be solved, however, He created other opportunities for us to eventually solve our dilemma. What is important here is that the student persevered, while asking our Higher Power for assistance. This occurred when the new student quickly began opening the pages of the newspaper, as karma somehow made sure that He happened to read the 'want ads' carefully enough, to discover this new job. Our Higher Power did not allow him to fail, since the new student persisted until he found a solution that worked. As it is written, "For the one who asks, receives. The one who seeks, finds. The one who knocks, enters."

Chapter 21: Alice

I wish to live my gentle and peacefully centered life, according to what our Higher Power and His Son have expressed to me through their Words and their actions. I must also not allow others, who have contrasting belief systems, to deter me from my own faith, even though, it would be advantageous to listen to their point of view. Other people have noticed that I appear at ease and content, which is completely due to having discovered my inner peace, as this has allowed my soul and my mind to become comforted, and filled with feelings of well-being. Others may attempt to discourage me from my own spirituality; therefore, I must sensitively and methodically defend my beliefs, which have been sacredly inspired, even though there is a great benefit to reading books concerning other major religions of the world. I once heard a heart-breaking story about a woman named Alice, who was a young mother of three children. Alice was unfortunately addicted to narcotics, while selling them on a street corner, in order to make money for her family. She was eventually caught by the police, and went to prison for this crime. While in prison, she came to the realization that her usage of these damaging substances, did more than just injure her mind and body; they harmed her spirit as well. She understood that her soul had been struggling lately, since she had practiced a Christian-based religion, earlier on in life. Alice promised herself, that she would never again, take another recreational drug. During her term in prison, she was inspired to pray and read her Bible, which the prison chaplain had provided to her earlier. The inmates always observed that she had a Bible in her hands. As it is written, "Blest are the single-hearted for they shall see God." As she became more faithful to God, she appeared to be more at ease, as feelings of serenity and of quiet pleasure, permeated her consciousness. The rest of the women in prison also enjoyed her gentleness, since it also gave them a sense of peace. She was a bright light which radiated against the darkened prison walls, as she became amiable with the prisoners and the guards alike. She allowed her natural goodness to shine through her vibrant personality. Alice and the prison chaplain came together for weekly Bible studies, as he answered her questions and listened to her comments. Even though the chaplain did not belong to any particular Christian denomination, he seemed to be a Bible Scholar, and also understood the tenets, of some of the other major religions of the world. For example, He had Religious Scripture and Sacred Texts of: The Quran (Islamic), the Written Torah (Jewish), and the Sutras (Buddhist). She relished her time with the prison chaplain, since he was so well versed in the Bible. Later that day, there was a woman prisoner who came to offer her 'friendship' to Alice, subsequent to meeting her in the prison yard a few days earlier. Unfortunately, this woman did not have Alice's best interest at heart, because she offered her a free hit of heroin. Alice began to stutter and was visibly shaken, as she became powerless over the entire situation. She was not prepared for this predicament, as this situation was clearly overwhelming. Her response was a frenzied one, as it did not take Alice any time to fold under the pressure. Alice struggled, as she grabbed the heroin from the other woman's hand, pressed the needle in her arm, and quickly propelled the heroin inside of her vein. This entire interaction was completed before the guard could turn around, and therefore, they were not caught. Sadly, 'Alice's friend' knew that this heroin would give her a high that she could not ignore, and as a result of this one hit, she became addicted again, and would now have to purchase heroin in prison; probably from 'her new friend.' Alice's faith was not quite strong enough, to release her from the desire of wanting, and actually needing this heroin. She did not hesitate in the least, when she quickly seized the needle from the other inmate. As we know, no one is exempt from the prince of darkness and his trappings; not even Jesus, as the devil said to Him, "If you are the Son of God, throw yourself down. Scripture has it: 'He will bid his angels take care of you; with their hands they will support you that you may never stumble on a stone.'" "Jesus answered him, 'Scripture also has it: You shall not put the Lord your God to the test,'" as it is written. Our Higher Power allows us to be tested by the prince of darkness, just as His Son was tested. This in turn, gave our

Higher Power a sense of how strong our faith was, as it remained with us. Alice was unsuccessful this time, since she did not pass the test. Until this very day, Alice remains out of prison, on the streets, and has fallen back into her old lifestyle. I believe that if she would not have met that 'friend' in prison, she might have been sober today, however, she allowed the complexities of drug misuse, to fail her. Let us not tolerate harmful people in our lives, who can unwittingly exchange our beacon of light, for darkened obscurity and pain. Taking either heroin or other narcotics chronically, has become her largest downfall. Substance addiction is rampant and may also occur within our own lives. Therefore, let us remain vigilant, so that we may warn ourselves when the prince of darkness comes near. Studies show, that more than fifty percent of the women in prison, remain as inmates for abusing and/or selling drugs. I humbly believe, that these women would have a better chance at ending their drug abuse, if they were placed in a detox center, with a program that had a specific agenda for each individual. This is where a medical doctor could provide these women with counseling and medications, as they would work towards finally conquering their addictions.

Chapter 22: Forgiveness

Forgiveness is an exceptional gift, which is given to us by The Holy Spirit. We should utilize this inspirational gift, when someone either abuses us physically, or alleges something unkind towards us. When there is someone we need to forgive, our resentment begins to discharge like lava, streaming from a volcano. His Son wants us to calmly and mercifully pardon our offender, even though this may be distasteful. Most times, the offender will not apologize for his actions, however, if he does, the tone in which the apology has been delivered, has much to do with how the innocent party will choose to either forgive, or remain without forgiving his aggressor. His Son, however, is asking us not to make that distinction within the apology's tonality. In fact, He wants us to forgive the offender, even though he has not chosen to render an apology to us, at all. Deep within our soul, forgiveness becomes a time-sensitive matter for a few reasons. The most important reason is due to our lack of knowledge; meaning that we do not know when our last moments on earth will occur, and we may not have enough time left, prior to our demise, in order to forgive our offender. Granting another soul's forgiveness is necessary for our own soul to be forgiven. When sinners ask for absolution, this request will be immediately satisfied, just as Jesus has promised us, except if there are exigent circumstances. Some of these circumstances include: 1) asking for absolution with a non-repentant heart, or 2) simply not asking for absolution at all. The offender might have asked for forgiveness from the innocent person he had harmed; however, he must also ask His Son for His forgiveness. I believe the adage is, 'forgive and forget;' have we truly forgiven the offender if we cannot forget his deed? I do not believe so, since it is impossible to separate the sin, which we must forgive, from the suffering, which we must forget, as it is impossible to control what our mind will recall at certain times. Therefore, every time we experience the offender's crassness or ignorance with any of our sensibilities, we may remember how the sinner's indiscretion has affected us. This may bring up thoughts and feelings of anger and pain, once again. Pardoning the offender who has harmed us, should be of monumental concern, as our Higher Power does not tolerate anger from any of us. As it is written, "Everyone who grows angry with his brother shall be liable to judgment...." He allows us the ability to extinguish this angry feeling instantly, and helps us choose to forgive and forget. As a result, we will feel unburdened and freed. As it is written, "Blest are they who show mercy; mercy shall be theirs." It is better to emote the sense of freedom we have received from pardoning our offender, than to feel tightly wound inside, while we are not willing to excuse him just yet; as we are the ones who truly suffer from this procrastination. If we become sluggish in releasing our culprit from his malevolent act, then we could become a prime target for the prince of darkness, since he would alter our positive relationship with our Higher Power. As it is written, "If you forgive the faults of others, your heavenly Father will forgive you yours." I understand that the manner in which we live on earth, will in turn be identical to how the Son will judge us, subsequent to our demise. Our Higher Power is invariably around us, so that the prince of darkness will not take advantage of our hateful misjudgments, nor take advantage of our negligence, as we should forgive the hateful words or the harmful action which the offender has executed against us. Jesus knows our hearts and minds, so that if our tone is one of solemn repentance, as we converse with and confess to Him daily, then we should anticipate the replacement of our anger, with sympathy and genuine love.

Chapter 23: Love Your Enemies

"My command to you is: love your enemies, pray for your persecutors" as it is written. At times, His teachings demonstrate brevity and conciseness, and yet, the execution of these teachings are quite formidable, such as we will discover in this chapter. When this particular instruction was written in Scripture, the early Christians would go to battle for our Savior and the Christian religion, both with words and actions, as the non-Christians remained their persecutors, and desired to intentionally harm them. I find that in the twenty-first century, when the meanings of the words, enemies and persecutors are used, both have less brutal connotations, then when Jesus and His apostles walked on earth, since people often killed their enemies and persecutors. The words enemy and persecutor have similar meanings; however, they are not identical. The word enemy connotes: antagonism, opposition, and contrarianism, signifying that our enemies possess opposing viewpoints on various issues, as our enemies refuse to spend any time with us, because they see matters through different-colored glasses. The word persecutor connotes: maltreatment, abuse, injury, and molestation, meaning that our persecutor's hatred is exhibited when they strike us, due to how we act, or of what we speak. Both words signify a type of oppression. Let us recall that our Higher Power loves our enemies and persecutors, as much as He loves us. Let us always attempt to completely comprehend how we discern, and then observe Christ within our enemies. I realize that this is one of His Son's most radical teachings, however, we must love others with the same love that our Higher Power has for our enemies. This does not signify that we must love someone for whom we already have a friendly affection, since these people are easy for us to love. No, He declares that we should truly love our enemies, as He does. Let us remember, ...'You shall love your neighbor as yourself,' as it is written. This appears to be difficult at first, however, practice, as you will indeed surprise yourself in a good way. Let us remember to love ourselves; since, when we reach this goal, we can love others. Some of our enemies simply pass us by and laugh, whether we are in public or in private, as they quickly decide that they dislike us for their own reasons. We are asked to love them, even though they have mentally abused and puzzled us. The quote at the beginning of this chapter, takes on a new life, if we discuss our religious beliefs with our enemies. Since we end up on opposing sides, when we declare that we depend upon a strong faith in Jesus, and they do not, then these few words may turn this discourse into a dispute, as our enemies may quickly become our persecutors. Unfortunately, this happens on a grand scale, such as we unfortunately observe in Israel and Palestine today, as they have been fighting a 'holy war' for many years. When we begin to explore the love, which we shall innately pursue and give to our enemies, we may make a misstep by starting not to care for them, as we might simply finish our journey by having no feelings, whatsoever, towards our enemies. We may try to fool ourselves by possessing this nonchalant attitude, since having absolutely no feelings for someone, as we may attempt to block these feelings within our minds, can be categorized as a type of hatred. Let us, therefore, be cautious, as it is necessary to be vigilant, when searching for the love we will eventually maintain, for our enemies. I do not believe that we should become angry with the opposition, due to the fact that our persecutors and enemies remain precious to our Higher Power. They remain precious, simply due to the treasure we all carry within us from Heaven, as we all continue to be children of God. This information helps us to progressively and eventually love our enemies; although this love, deep within our souls, may take some time to fully develop. Let Him punish our enemies and persecutors, as we should not perform this ourselves, since we are not their creators. I continue to pray for our Higher Power's guidance, as we endeavor to alter the opposition's thinking pattern, which will mend their maladjusted hatred towards us and others; only if this incident truly becomes His will. One of the significant issues is our maltreatment, which our persecutors impose upon us, due to the ideologies we support. They should simply treat us in the manner in which they wish to be treated. We need to rise above our opposition, since our intuition reminds us that we should seek Him first, and only then, may we share some of our own love with them. Let us be the voice of reason and tranquility, just as He is the Voice of our moral code. It may also be feasible and reasonable to expect that we might speak to our enemies regarding what their problem is with us, and then, we may have the capability of solving our differences with them. Our message shall be sent to the opposition, out of love, as the enactment of such love will always triumph. We will either pursue our precious Higher Power's desire for mercy and love, or we will needlessly follow the dark force's proclivity into his vicious world of degradation and defiance. Let us keep mercy and love as our shields against our enemies' and persecutor's comments and behaviors, as we should never be bitter towards our enemies, and never be in doubt of our faith, nor in the power of our love.

Chapter 24: Sign of the Cross

As I invariably commence my prayer with the sign of the cross, I know that this gesture will elicit His blessing upon His faithful daughter, and keep me safe from the foolish and foolhardy prince of darkness. I try never to bless myself in a flippant-like manner, even if I am in a hurry or late to mass. This sacred gesture blesses all of us, who perform the sign of the cross with a purpose, which signifies that we are ready to be with His Son in a profound way. As I gently, and intentionally make this holy gesture, I hold the gaze of Christ in my mind, just as if I was at His crucifixion, looking into His eyes, approximately two thousand years ago. I notice His angelic head anchoring a crown of thorns, as beads of sweat and blood begin to trickle down His face. He stares back at me hanging from His cross, as if to say, 'My heart is filled with sadness, since I must deliver myself over to death for your sins, and the sins of others.' Subsequent to finishing my prayers, I must then focus on what my intuition affirms, as a message answering my prayers may be given to me by our Heavenly Father or His Son. This occurs through the flow of telepathic energy, as this type of energy is translated into the feelings we gather within our intuition, and is then further translated into our specific human language, as the energy travels upwards and reaches our minds. We know that praying does not signify that we must always be busy speaking, since we must be silent for some of the time, in order to listen to our intuition. We must then, formulate an idea from what our intuition discloses to us. When I picture our Higher Power in my consciousness, I imagine Him to be an Entity who exists everywhere, as He acts as a highly organized quantum of unknown energy. As it is written, "He was still speaking when suddenly a bright cloud overshadowed them. Out of the cloud came a voice which said, 'This is my beloved Son on whom my favor rests. Listen to him.'" We have not been given the capability of discerning or comprehending His presence within the cloud, since He is invisible to us, just as energy is invisible. The effects of energy are most apparent, just as His actions and the consequences of His actions are also apparent. Maybe we are not meant to decipher this enigma, just yet, however, our inquisitiveness is a rather strong characteristic which we wish to apply to this situation, so that we may comprehend as much as we can about, and from our Higher Power, although, this cannot be possible until Jesus arrives on earth for the last time. The beautiful wonderment which He created for us, has captured our sense of amazement and curiosity, however, we have not been fully appeased nor felt fully at ease, since He is simply inexplicable, as we function with knowledge that causes us to be dissatisfied, since there are many mysteries that we are not privileged to understand currently. Our knowledge will in effect continue to be denied, until the second coming of His Son, which is when we may learn more, about the three Entities.

Chapter 25: Seeking My Higher Power

If we are prepared to grab our lives, and live them to the fullest, without the benefit of our Father's assistance and direction, we will certainly regret these actions. We may think that by making decisions on our own, we show how powerful and intelligent we are, however, let us not be so ill-advised, as to adhere to this self-righteous thinking, since it is far from the truth. I believe that we should never foolishly discount our Higher Power's indispensable advice, concerning the navigation of our lives. At times, we tend to proceed by forming our own judgment, without any reflection upon His Words. His Words will ease our anxiety, as we are often called to make many difficult decisions, during our lifetime. The truth is that we never stand alone, and our influence upon the present, shall not be executed without Him. After all, we are God's children, and He desires what is best for us, therefore, let us joyfully and completely include Him in our life; not only for the problems He helps us to decipher, but to simply open the window to our essence, and allow His love and solicitude to pour forth into our blessed soul. I have a good friend, who is pregnant and struggles with the ideas of abortion and adoption. Even though she is somewhat spiritual, she has requested that I help her during this time in her life. Since I have sought His assistance first, I feel that God has been guiding my intuition, as it remains open to Him, and ready for further suggestions. As we discuss abortion and adoption, I must quietly listen to my own intuition, as I will eventually lead my friend in the proper direction, with God's counsel. Her choices are: bearing her child and keeping him, giving-up her rights to an adoptive couple, leaving her baby in foster care, or aborting her fetus. Even though our Higher Power is fully cognizant of which of the four choices my friend will select, she must still form one of these decisions; for herself and for her child. I pray that she remains peaceful with the support of our Higher Power; especially during her pregnancy. I will disclose to her that God has been leading both of us, during this difficult time in her life. I humbly believe, that if she would only ask Him to be at the helm of her ship, then she would not have to struggle so much with this conundrum. We can remain certain, that we may guide our friend today, since I am confident that He has already guided me in the proper direction. Another example of a life or death circumstance occurred in the New Testament, when His Son agonized in the garden, as He declared, "Abba (O Father), you have the power to do all things. Take this cup away from me. But let it be as you would have it, not as I," as it is written. In this Scripture, we discover that His Son speaks with His Father in the garden, since He is in dire need of His comfort and support. As we recall, His Father did not take this most difficult "cup away" from His Son. Our Higher Power actively guides our decisions, if He has been asked to do so by any one of us, and sometimes He guides us, even though we have not asked Him to do so. Although, we attempt to remain peaceful, we cannot, as we yearn for His direction, and desperately need Him to be our helmsman, as He advises our intuition, and further helps us to make the correct choices and decisions, if we allow Him in our lives. As we remain cognizant that we are simply doing what He requires, this action, which genuinely gives Him feelings of content, will give us tremendous peace and relief. Let us place ourselves in our Higher Power's capable and gentle hands. He is omnipotent as He sees everything we do, and therefore, we should ask Him to breathe His Truths and wishes, into the solutions of our dilemmas, as this will keep us righteous and tranquil in our lives. Lastly, my good friend gave her baby up for adoption to a lovely couple.

Chapter 26: Saints/Prayer

As it is written, "Pray perseveringly, be attentive to prayer, and pray in a spirit of thanksgiving. Pray for us, too, that God may provide us with an opening to proclaim the mystery of Christ, for which I am a prisoner. Pray that I may speak it clearly, as I must. Be prudent in dealing with outsiders; make the most of every opportunity. Let your speech be always gracious and in good taste, and strive to respond properly to all who address you." This quote declares, how all of us should pray, as well as, how all of us should act. We welcome the prayers that others say for us, just as we have said prayers for others. If God gives us a chance to inform non-believers about Christ's saving power, let us speak knowingly regarding His merciful judgment of our souls. When speaking with others, let us make sure that we are always courteous and gentle, and let us attempt to speak righteously with others, who call out to us. Personally, I do pray to our Higher Power and His Son, since I wish to be absolved of my sins, and wish to cultivate a meaningful relationship with both the Father and 'Christ the King.' One on one communication is the purest, and the most coherent form of our discussion with Him, as it is the most expressive method by which we can pray. There are many people in this world, who possess a great faith in the workings of the saints, as they do not wish to converse with the Entities of the Complete Being; one on one. These individuals firmly believe that the saint they love, respect, and pray to, shall deliver their prayers to our Higher Power with more urgency and effectiveness; as if these prayers were 'highlighted' and had the ability to travel to the 'head of the line' more quickly. I humbly believe, that the saints do maintain a special bond with our Higher Power, as they have performed miracles under His guardianship on earth. I firmly believe, however, that the saints do not have the capability in advancing our prayers to Him, since praying to our Higher Power directly, consists of fulfilling a solemn connection into which no one else should enter, as we possess the unparalleled privilege of having solely unique conversations with Him. These are multiple blessed moments, which have been gifted to us, by God. If we believe, that praying through one saint will assist us in reaching our Higher Power, then maybe we should consider asking all of the saints to intervene on our behalf. Some of us continue to believe that these cherished and beloved sainted souls, effect the exigent nature of our prayers to our Higher Power and His Son. Let us not squander our petitions by imploring a saint to pass our prayers onto Him, since I humbly believe that saints do not have the capability to receive our prayers, in order to deliver them to God. Why would He need an intercessor, when we telepathically communicate our prayers to Him? Our prayers can only fully be accepted, and reflected upon, by the Entities of the Complete Being. Some of us feel, that since the saints are closer within a spatial relationship, and within a spiritual connection to our Higher Power, these saints may bring a more tender passion to our message and our prayers, since the saints know Him better. Even though I understand why these certain people feel the way they do, I cannot disagree with this sentiment more. I believe that our prayers will instead be lovingly accepted by the Entities, straight from our lips, or from our thoughts. What possible role can a saint fulfill, during our continuous and sacred relationship between God and us? Certainly, these saints can compel a greater relationship between our Higher Power and us, since the saints we respect, may function as catalysts, which help us to imitate the virtue that they displayed throughout their lives, as we learn their stories by reading interesting biographies about them. Although we love our saints, we should not pray to them as if they were a deity, since they are more like mentors. This love reminds me of the saint I most admire; we know her as Saint (Mother) Teresa of Kolkata, who was canonized in the year 2016. I will not pray to her, nor request her to pray for me, since He is 'our' Higher Power for a good reason, which is that He wishes to hear from each of us. There is no time involved when we express our prayers to Him, since He has always known what we desire, and therefore, we should examine our intuition and listen to His Word, as this will help us to flourish and to remain innately peaceful. Let us deliver our distinctive prayers with ease, love, and humility, as these prayers shall directly be sent from us, His children, to our Heavenly Father, through telepathic communication, which was given to us by The Holy Spirit. We know that praying allows us to completely understand and validate our ideas, by coordinating our thoughts and emotions upon the issues we choose to communicate, thereby carving out our own beautiful connection and dependence upon our Higher Power. God may entice us to converse with Him, by giving us a situation to resolve; however, we may not have the capability to solve it, and therefore, we will need His assistance, as we communicate our pleas and prayers to Him. Let us continue to strive to be like the saints we love, since they have brought immense compassion and goodness into our world, as they have garnered a special relationship with our Father; just as we all have done, in our own unique way.

Chapter 27: Poems

Even though we are capable of sharing our thoughts, such as in a Bible study or with a true friend, the circumstances that genuinely satisfy our souls and minds, are the private conversations we continue to maintain with the Entities of the Complete Being. A wonderful way to connect with our Higher Power, is to first write a few lines of poetry; especially if our focus on Him has gone awry. Poetry can mitigate the chaos which permeates our minds. As we start to concentrate on one particular word at a time, these words eventually turn into verses, as this mental exercise enables us to feel fulfilled and at ease. Subsequent to our writings, time leisurely lingers just enough, so that we may now successfully return to praying and conversing with our Higher Power, or another Entity. For example, I wrote both of these little poems, while I had an exceptionally troublesome time, following-through and completing one of my conversations with Him:

The Ocean

Following a seagull, gliding towards the ocean,
Standing and watching, with delightful emotion,

Waves that pass, smooth as glass, over and over,
Causing the beat of life, to gently stir down under,

Life flourishes, in the majestic blue ocean,
The moon arouses the tides, onward forward motion,

Waves which could propel me far, far astray,
Where would I land, where would I stay?

This peacefulness may occur in my reality,
However, it could all just be imaginary; ahh...

The Sacred Trinity

As I continue to meditate upon the Holy Trinity,
I find that I gather thoughts about a Sacred Entity,

The Father, the Son, and The Holy Spirit; all in one,
Love envelops me; my pondering shall never be done,

As I continue to pray, and search for a solution,
Be not with the devil; he forms fires and causes confusion,

No more do I need to walk the face of the earth alone,
The Trinity has now given me comfort and a home,

As I know that our God is within my soul,
I shall fill it with love and faith as I grow old,

However, when I am down, and my light is dim,
I shall invite Him in, and simply listen...

Chapter 28: The Denial

We should always want to do what is righteous in God's eyes. Let us, therefore, pay close attention, as He guides us regarding how our lives may enter and remain on a pathway of virtue, which will then lead us to our inner peace. Our Higher Power even grants us the opportunity to deny His wishes, as He has supplied each of His children with a free will, which we may use to unfortunately fail Him, and fail ourselves. Even though we have cogitated upon, how to pursue and finally acquire our inner peace, this is vastly different than actually executing these wishes, to His satisfaction. Our good intentions can be transformed into denials, since we may not have carried out His wishes, performed in His way, and therefore, we will have denied Him. Even though we have abandoned Him, He refuses to abandon us. God sees us, as we have become discouraged and disconcerted, since we have failed Him, however, even though He is displeased with us for a moment, He refuses to resent us. Let us reclaim our inner peace, as we attempt to remain on a straight path, and discover that by making Him content, we shall also become content. He knows that what He asks of us will be difficult to fulfill, as we are the ones who allow our guilt to needlessly remove ourselves from our communication with Him. Let us remain connected to Him, no matter how many times we fail, since He has never pushed us away. We are safe, as long as we continue our spiritual life, guided by our Higher Power, as He holds each of us in His comforting arms, especially when we become depressed and downcast. Personally, I have had many good intentions, but have failed to achieve what He wanted me to accomplish, since I allowed my worldly distractions to whisk me away, as these distractions superseded His spiritual desires for my soul. At times, we shun Him because He has already answered our prayers, and therefore, we needlessly forgot or thought that it was unnecessary to communicate with Him, until we needed Him again. We should not continue to reject Him, just because our senseless reasoning has covered our good and proper thoughts, as we should connect with our Higher Power many times during each day. Our senseless reasoning takes place when a veil of obscurity covers our good ideas, and allows our bad ideas to come to the forefront. For instance, this occurs when we spend more time managing our secular lives, than our spiritual lives. This rejection has also happened to His Son, at the hands of Peter, the disciple, whose denial was foretold. Jesus said to him, "I give you my word, before the cock crows tonight you will deny me three times." Peter replied, "Even though I have to die with you, I will never disown you..." as it is written. Peter did eventually deny the Son three times, before the cock crowed. Peter continued to deny Him, even when the Savior asked Peter to remain awake with Him, during the agony in the garden. When Jesus returned from praying with His Father in the garden, He found Peter asleep, and He was disturbed that Peter could not stay awake with Him for even an hour. Before Jesus was arrested, all of the disciples, including Peter, fled, which showed us that we all suffer with either denying our Lord by our statements, or denying our Lord by the actions we fulfill. The Savior, even having the full knowledge that Peter would indeed deny Him at a later date, had previously informed Peter, that he would be the 'cornerstone of His church.' Let us keep trying, as we hope to achieve what He wants us to accomplish, in the end. Personally, I have denied Him myself, just as Peter had done. As I happened to be walking down the street, I began silently expressing an impromptu prayer, and sensed that I wished to make the sign of the cross, as my prayer came to a conclusion. I, however, refused to do so, as I did not want to embarrass myself in public, since I did not desire to be thought of as a religious zealot, nor did I wish to encroach on anyone else's religious beliefs. When I finally caught myself continuing to deny His Son through my aversion, I made certain that this aversion would prevail for the last time. I am aware that my refusal to bless myself had been happening for years, and being embarrassed of this most sacred ritual, meant that I was embarrassed of my Savior. At that moment, I suddenly felt deflated and greatly saddened, as my aversion was not a revelation in any sense. I immediately received an impression through my intuition, that He was not pleased with me, since I had avoided His Son, however, I understood that I should not mistreat myself for this blunder, since I can alter this erroneous course, by invariably blessing myself with the sign of the cross, whenever I end a prayer. Let us do what is important to Him and His Son, as we remain in communication with them, instead of worrying about the displeasure, which we have sent forth, into the cosmos, regarding our own missteps. It is more of a necessity to be in communion with the Entities, then it is to use this energy to turn away from our Lord. The sorrow which we have caused will always be seen as a failure and as a denial of our God, however, let us remain confident in our Higher Power and His Son since they have promised us unconditional love, no matter how many times we fail. Even though we feel discouraged and dismayed, He says that we should not be, as we should shelter ourselves from these feelings, and perform the sacrifices and deeds He has asked us to complete. We must keep trying, since He expects all of us to try, however, He does not expect all of us to achieve.

Chapter 29: Sacrifices

There is beauty in sacrifice and suffering, for if an individual does not attempt to end his suffering, this shows his submission to our Higher Power, as he places his life in our Heavenly Father's firm, and gentle hands. We are blessed by our Higher Power, when we make sacrifices and offer them for the benefit of our neighbors, who are in need of some respite and peace, as they currently live with their daily pain and injustice. When we pray and offer our sacrifices up to our Higher Power for others, He alters our suffering into a well-deserved gift of relief. The feelings we enjoy, when we give of ourselves in sacrifice, are palpable. Having sacrificed, we have been through an experience, which no one can take away from us. The sacrificial mind is a profound mind, since we must find comfort in the Lord, instead of in materialistic items. We will also find it necessary to lean upon others, because at one time or another, we will also be in need of our neighbors' sacrifices and prayers. Let us listen to our sensitive inclinations and our intuition, so that we may be given the gift of suffering to help our brothers and sisters, at the appropriate moment. At times, prodding ourselves to make a sacrifice, even when we are not mentally prepared to do so, is considered an even greater sacrifice. When we make a sacrifice, it is unnecessary to lament about having to give-up a certain substance, or an object that we enjoy. The reason being is that we may solely continue to make our sacrifice, in order to garner some attention and respect from others; an action which God does not support. If we merely disclose our self-denial to a friend, just for informational purposes, such as answering our friend's question regarding why we refuse to eat our favorite food at the restaurant today, then our answer will completely be copacetic. It is all in the way in which we frame our information, and use the proper words in our disclosure. If, however, we divulge that we are suffering due to our self-denial, and our friend consoles us, then God will probably not accept this gift of sacrifice from us, since we have already received our gift of solace and sympathy. As it is written, "The spirit is willing but our nature is weak..." What is truly at the core of our mind, is the deciding factor, for whether He will accept, or deny our sacrifice. As for myself, I humbly believe that my sacrifice is personal; as my sacrifice is not for anyone else to discover, nor to perceive how I cope with my spiritual endeavor. Upon close study, I find that I have a deeper faith during the struggle of self-denial, then when I am not executing any sacrifices, during the same period of time. Our sacrifice places us emotionally closer to His Son, since the feelings of self-denial binds us. Our sacrifice penetrates and damages our emotions of comfortability and contentment, as we learn to surrender and yearn for Him. His Son demonstrated to us how dutifully He conducted Himself, while agonizing through the preparation of His crucifixion. We should learn to emulate His actions, as He has made many sacrifices during His lifetime on earth. Jesus is known to us by the term, 'Sacrificial Lamb,' as a result of His sacrificial death for us. We should endure our sacrifice in an environment created by pondering celestial matters, more so than that of worldly matters, as this will bestow some newly-found connections, which travel from our souls and minds, to our Higher Power and His Son. A season of sacrifice helps us to sympathize with our neighbors who: go hungry, live with pain, live with loneliness, or live with depression. Our sacrifice, not that I wish to detract from it, does not rise to the level of those who remain impoverished or suffer daily. We possess the ability to terminate our sacrifice at any moment, whereas the destitute do not have this option. Let us pray and sacrifice ourselves for the, "Least of my brothers." Lent is a time period in which all of us are invited to deny ourselves of substances, or circumstances we enjoy, as we may require the struggle of our offering to be donated as a prayer for others, who are destitute, lack spiritual guidance, remain depressed, or suffer with great pain. Lent exists for forty days and forty nights; from Ash Wednesday to Easter Sunday, every year. The number forty is a repetitive number, since this number is written and used in the Sacred Scripture many times, including: Genesis, Exodus, and Acts. This number occurs most importantly during the Gospels of the New Testament, as we may remember His Son's sacrifice, as He traveled through the desert, fasting and communicating with His Father, for forty days and forty nights. Sacrifice is good for our souls, as we should not always have everything we need, since this helps us to journey inwards, and expand upon the realization that we must find peace and happiness within ourselves, and within God. We, I believe, shall instantly understand that this realization, must be completely based upon our communication with our Higher Power and His Son. This sacrifice helps us to comprehend and commiserate with the indigent, the poor who lack spiritual guidance, and other individuals who need our assistance. If we have everything we want or need, why should we have the impetus to seek-out His mercy and love? Let us continue to make sacrifices for our neighbors, as we will find that we are also enriched, by our own endeavors.

Chapter 30: Personal Accountability

As it is written, "I will entrust to you the keys of the kingdom of heaven. Whatever you declare bound on earth shall be bound in heaven; whatever you declare loosed on earth shall be loosed in heaven."   In the Book of Matthew, Jesus is solely speaking to His disciple, Peter, when He discloses these words to him.   Later in the Book of Matthew, however, His Son actually reiterates the same words to each of His twelve apostles, who continue to spread the news to other towns about His Words, and therefore, we have all become His new apostles, by these actions. What Jesus reveals to us is that He truly relies upon each of us for our own commitment to Him, since we remain the guardians of our own soul and in possession of our own reality, as God has given us a free will. Each of us lives through various circumstances and consequences, which shape our view of life itself, and therefore, our declarations of what is bound and what is loosed, may be somewhat different for each of us, as this quote applies to every one of us. For instance, all of us do not worship within the same religion, and so, our belief and our insight to what may be sinful, may not be quite the same as another individual's belief and his insight, because both individuals may worship within different religions, and therefore, have differing holy texts.   We each have the ability to comprehend which of our words and actions will either open or close the proverbial door to Heaven, as we shall each take personal accountability for the things we say or do here on earth. The word "bound," translates into being restrained and secured, which in this context signifies "sinful." The word "loosed," translates into being freed and undone, as it also means, "sinless." The entirety of this quote signifies that: whatever we consider to be a sin on earth, shall exist as a sin in Heaven, as we must be forgiven for this action; and whatever we consider to be pure and well-intentioned on earth, shall be deemed pure and well-intentioned in Heaven. We all have unique footprints or patterns of sinfulness, which are indelibly marked upon our souls, unless we have been forgiven for these sins. There are two quotes within the Scripture which richly supports the theory of personal accountability. As it is written, "If you forgive the faults of others, your heavenly Father will forgive you yours," and "If you want to avoid judgment, stop passing judgment," as it is written. As each of us progresses towards being *Peacefully Centered*, life on this earth remains a test, which we must endure. If we pass certain trials, by listening to what our Higher Power desires of us, and accepting Jesus, by understanding what He has graciously brought into our lives, such as His undying mercy and love, then our reward shall not only include our inner peace, but it shall also include the Kingdom of Heaven. Heaven will become our destination; however, this will only happen if Jesus, through His merciful judgment, perceives the strength of our faith as being consistent and vigorous. How we witness and react to the circumstances in our world will be inspected by our Higher Power, since He hears the words we declare, and sees the actions we execute. Some of the differences in the attitudes we present are due to our family and our neighborhood, as we each grew-up in different environments and various circumstances. We, however, are now adults, and are completely responsible for our own words and actions during this lifetime, as personal accountability is an important theme, which is embedded in our Savior's Covenant with each of us.

Chapter 31: Rebekah

Let us for a moment, delve into the year 1500 B.C., as we separate ourselves from our own spiritual beliefs, and instead try to understand what a middle-aged Jewish woman, named Rebekah, experiences as she discloses her feelings when she writes in her journal, regarding her own existence. Since Rebekah lives in 1500 B.C., she does not have access to a Bible, because the entire Holy Scripture was written between 1200 B.C. and 120 A.D. Let us attempt to comprehend Rebekah's spirit, as she follows Moses and the Israelites out of Egypt and into the desert. As they come upon Mt. Sinai, God summons Moses to the top of the mountain, where He discloses the Ten Commandments, and declares that He shall be called, Lord. During the days the Israelites remain camped-out at the base of Mt. Sinai, Moses becomes the conduit between what the Lord expects from the Israelites, and what the Israelites wish to inquire about the Lord. One of the Israelites basically said, 'Why does thunder, lightning, and a loud trumpet blast resonate from the mountain top? These occurrences completely frighten all of us.' As it is written, Moses said, "Do not be afraid, for God has come to you only to test you and put his fear upon you, lest you should sin." God, on this journey, strictly speaks to Moses, and when our Higher Power imparts His Laws upon the Israelites, they declare to Moses, "We will do everything that the Lord has told us," as it is written. The Lord then summons Moses to the top of Mt. Sinai once again, as he disappears from the Israelites for forty days and forty nights. Rebekah is a simple woman who once had a loving husband, however, he died as a slave in Egypt, prior to the exodus. At first glimpse, we find Rebekah questioning Moses' disappearance, as she begins to write in her journal, 'The daily struggle of my spiritually confused life is wearisome. I hope that I can trust that this is the God of all; the God of Adam and Eve, and the God of the one who is to come. Even though this God remains hidden by fire and smoke, at the top of Mt. Sinai, I believe in Him since Moses also believes.' After the Lord is through speaking with

Moses, He gives him the two tablets, which are once again inscribed by His finger. The Israelites begin to be dismayed, as they are tired of waiting for Moses, since he has not yet arrived at base camp for some time. Rebekah opens her journal to her previous entry, and declares, 'We only see a consuming fire and bellowing smoke, as our Moses walked through this smoke, disappeared, and has yet to come back to us. What has happened to him; has he died?' When Moses finally arrives at base camp, he speaks to the Israelites with a firm tone in his voice, regarding the grave sin they had perpetrated. Moses tells them to atone for the golden calf which they had erected, as they worshipped this calf like a god. Moses continues to disclose, that they are to build an ark, which would become a dwelling and a place to transport the Lord, as the Israelites planned to continue on their journey. Rebekah flips through her journal one last time, as she writes, 'I wonder if there is truly a spiritual life beyond this life, and what would a life within the heavens be like? Would we all exist in a different realm with Moses' God; the God of all? As I continue to think about the possibility of having another life besides this one, I am sure that the news of an existence beyond what we experience here, would ignite a vibrancy and a genuine happiness within me, since the life I possess here is quite tiresome. I try to obey the Laws and Ordinances which God gave us, however, I happen to remain a sinner, such as my predecessors Adam and Eve. I was told by a prophet that the Voice once said to Adam, 'By the sweat of your face shall you get bread to eat, Until you return to the ground, from which you were taken; For you are dirt, and to dirt you shall return,' as it is written. I think about these Words, and I find that these Holy Words convince me that Adam came to life from dirt, and the Voice must have given him a spirit-life, as Adam was able to take a large gasp of air, and was transformed into a living being. When he took his last breath, he returned to the dirt where his body remained. Therefore, my question is, where did the spirit-life, which Adam was blessed with, return to after he died? Did it die too? I do not think so, since I have faith that Moses and Adam spoke with the same Voice. This must have been God Himself, and I realize that He does not solely worry about Moses. I believe that this life-force must be instilled within all of us, just as God had infused this life-force within Adam. I also now believe, that this spirit-life lives in us and beyond our mortal lives; however, where does it, or where do we, go? This allows me to enjoy a sense of hope, because if we do not have hope, we cannot envision an afterlife. Adam and Eve heard the Voice, just as plainly as my children hear me speak, as they, being of the next generation, also believe in certain celestial promises through some of our credible prophets. I plan to speak to the heavens and to our Lord, so that He may guide my family into an afterlife. I now believe in our God, the Lord of all, who will not leave our spirit-lives on earth, but will take them into the heavens, where He must live. I will forever bow down in prayer to our Lord; may He always remain with us.' By writing in her journal, she is capable of disentangling her feelings about the Lord, and now lives with complete faith in Him, and in her destiny. Let us never stop wondering, imagining, or listening to what our Higher Power declares, since He lays a straight and narrow path for us to follow, just as Moses had followed our Higher Power's path of specific desires. Let us be the Moses' of our generation, as we have the ability to lead others to their inner peace, with God's guidance.

Chapter 32: Holy Spirit

"The grace of the Lord Jesus Christ, and the love of God, and the fellowship of The Holy Spirit be with you all," as it is written. Fellowship can be successfully dissected and translated into these four synonyms: companionship, friendship, neighborliness, and cooperation. The Holy Spirit is inordinately solicitous, as He creates and delivers to us the grace, the talents, and the gifts, which we need in order to thrive. As it is written, "To each person the manifestation of the Spirit is given for the common good. To one the Spirit gives wisdom in discourse, to another the power to express knowledge. Through the Spirit one receives faith; by the same Spirit another is given the gift of healing, and still another miraculous powers. Prophecy is given to one; to another power to distinguish one spirit from another. One receives the gift of tongues, another that of interpreting the tongues. But it is one and the same Spirit who produces all these gifts, distributing them to each as he wills." The Holy Spirit is responsible for our seemingly innate spiritual connections to the Entities of the Complete Being, as He has given us the gift of telepathy, which we use to communicate with each of the three Entities. We are not even aware that we are using this most satisfying of gifts when we pray, although, we are absolutely certain that our Higher Power and His Son receive all of our prayers and petitions. Telepathy is the manner by which we spiritually communicate with the Entities, however, when our Higher Power wishes to converse with us, this communication is slightly more complex to achieve, since our human body remains unique in its design. Our brains communicate via neurotransmitters and complimentary receptor sites; this is basically how our thoughts are formed. Upon our births, He had already equipped us with these specific complimentary items, which appear within the neurons of our brain. When we receive a telepathic communication from Heaven, it first enters our soul, and allows us to feel one way more than another, as our intuition expresses itself. Once this is expressed, the telepathic communication within our soul, then travels transfigured, as we now have the ability to comprehend the message in our own language, when it reaches our brains.   Let us think of The Holy Spirit, as if He were: the gasoline in our cars, the strike of a match, or a sudden wind arriving out of nowhere. The Holy Spirit causes circumstances to occur; not necessarily the where, the when, the what, or the why of the situation; however, He dictates 'the how,' of how all communication occurs, from ourselves, to the three Entities.   The Holy Spirit is the driving force behind our telepathy, since He begins and continues to set our conversations with the Entities into motion, which continue to occur 'in the blink of an eye.' The Holy Spirit is much more than a messenger or a bearer of gifts and talents, as the word messenger can also translate into the word, 'apostle.' As we recall, the Son's original twelve apostles, who testified about His miracles, as well as the substance of His doctrine, were certainly not only His Son's messengers; they also performed miracles, and gave others the hope and the Truth about our Savior, Jesus. They actually lived through the reality of what it was like to be a Christian in a mostly non-Christian era, as many of them were beaten and stoned by the Jewish community, due to their Christian beliefs. The Holy Spirit also warns us that, when there are evil spirits lurking, these malevolent spirits want to discourage us from any relationship we have with the Entities of the Complete Being. The Holy Spirit, therefore, will enlighten us, so that we should not have to follow the prince of darkness, nor his flawed ideology. "It is the Spirit that gives us life…" as it is written. The Holy Spirit has impressed us, with His elegant workings.   Let us acknowledge The Holy Spirit, by simply conversing with Him, as we should not forget to thank Him for generously bestowing the gifts we have received from His miraculous hands.

Chapter 33: Original Sin/Baptism

Each of our souls are stained when we are born. The original transgression, which caused the blemish, was perpetrated against our Higher Power, by Adam and Eve. As they decided to listen to the prince of darkness, Adam and Eve did not heed the simple instructions that our Lord gave them. This action regrettably compromised an integral part of Adam and Eve's legacy, as new infants continue to be born spiritually linked to impurity. Why were we born tainted with this sin, and why must we share in this legacy of unwitting evil? I humbly believe, that being born with a tainted soul, shows us that since we are all human and essentially possess similar curiosities, possess similar impulses, perform similar actions, and possess a similar genetic composition, then we too would have eaten the fruit from the forbidden tree. We commit similar sins to Adam and Eve's primary sin. Even though He asks us to execute certain actions, similar to the action He asked Adam and Eve to perform, we in turn, execute a contradictory action, which creates a sin and stains our soul until we ask for absolution. Our Higher Power stated in the garden of Eden, that we should not listen to the voice of evil, as this shall be the downfall of all generations to come, until the end of the world. Our Higher Power punished Adam, Eve, and the prince of darkness for this iniquity, and this simple lesson, continues to teach each generation, that they should read Genesis and must listen to God when He speaks to us. Our Higher Power wants us to recall, that the stain which the primary sin delivers to all of us, is due to each one of our flesh-driven desires, which will ultimately lead us to our spiritual death, since some of our desires will lead us to sin against Him. As it is written, "It is obvious what proceeds from the flesh: lewd conduct, impurity, licentiousness, idolatry, sorcery, hostilities, bickering, jealousy, outburst of rage, selfish rivalries, dissensions, factions, envy, drunkenness, orgies and the like. I warn you, as I have warned you before: those who do such things will not inherit the kingdom of God!" These next two quotes solidify the notion that each of our souls were born tarnished; as it is written, "Indeed, in guilt was I born, and in sin my mother conceived me;" also, "Can a man be found who is clean of defilement? There is none, however short his days..." as it is written. How can this stain be removed from our souls? The ultimate sacrificial death, which His Son selflessly endured for us, did not wash our stain away, although, His death does cleanse Adam and Eve from their transgression. His Son had accepted death and resurrection in reciprocity for the ability to completely cleanse us, from our sins, however, since we did not commit the primary sin directly, the purification of each of the stains upon our souls, must be achieved through another way. Adam and Eve are ultimately the sinners, as they must ask for absolution in this matter, however, baptism will cleanse this stain from our soul, as our Higher Power spoke through the clouds, and intimated that He was pleased when His Son became baptized in the Jordan River. As it is written, "To sum up, then: just as a single offense brought condemnation to all men, a single righteous act brought all men acquittal and life. Just as through one man's disobedience all became sinners, so through one man's obedience all shall become just." This quote reflects, that the intentional action, executed by Adam, was then made right by the intentional action, executed by His Son. I believe that the "single righteous act" which "brought all men acquittal and life" has a double meaning. The first righteous act being His Son's crucifixion, and the second, being His Son's baptism in the Jordan River, which remains the catalyst for all others of the Christian faith to be baptized. In my humble opinion, there are certain religions which believe and practice the gift of baptism prematurely. Baptisms are sometimes performed on infants of merely three or four months old. The logic behind this early baptism is expressed for purely one reason. If an infant were to expire by some tragedy, then God would instantly capture the infant's soul in His gentle hands, and carry him into his Heavenly reward, since this infant would effectively be absent of sin. If an infant does not receive baptism at an early age, and matures into a young person, then this young adult must wish to be rid of the stain, which the primary sin has left upon his soul. Baptisms should be performed for those of us who are of proper age, and for those of us who have the ability to completely comprehend the authenticity of this ritual. Water is poured over us, as it not only acts as a symbol, however, it is clearly and genuinely our belief, that baptismal water remains utterly responsible for the cleansing of our soul. We are showing our Higher Power that we do understand the extreme importance that this stain has had upon our souls during our lives, as we must understand the legacy from which we come. The Son was baptized as an adult by John the Baptizer, and His soul was cleansed from the tarnish which had remained. John the Baptizer applied water to all of the townspeople, and recited a few prayers over each of them. The word baptize translates into cleanliness and purification. Grace, a gift from The Holy Spirit, is bestowed upon us at baptism, and produces a true renewal of our soul, which becomes devoid of this blemish, for the very first time. As Christians, we wholeheartedly maintain that our soul's stain is thoroughly purified and removed, during the time of our baptism.

Chapter 34: Death Row Inmate

As it is written, "...that Christ Jesus came into the world to save sinners. Of these I myself am the worst. But on that very account I was dealt with mercifully, so that in me as an extreme case, Jesus Christ might display all his patience, and I might become an example to those who would later have faith in him and gain everlasting life." This quote could have been said by someone who was clearly responsible for the murder of his fellow man. I happened to be pondering this situation for a psychology class, which I am taking at a community college. I have always been fascinated with how a person can cross the proverbial line, and actually kill another person. Could he have been born this way, so that killing someone else lives within his DNA, or did the environment in which he matured, help to delineate who he became? He may have refused to develop a love for our Higher Power, and felt powerful enough on his own, so that he was not in need of God, nor in need of anyone else. As I continue to write this scenario for my studies, I understand that murder is behind what causes many people to live in maximum-security facilities. Subsequent to his capture, this inmate will now have plenty of time to reflect upon his transgression, and therefore, if he has had any experience with spirituality, his beliefs should begin to surface and give him strength. Unfortunately, this man currently sits on death row, as my thoughts regarding death row begin to form. Remaining alive is a necessity for this inmate, since he must not solely ask the merciful Christ for absolution, but he must repent and regret his action, as this may indeed become a long process of sorts for him, if he has not yet repented. I believe that, he has the ability to maintain a better relationship with the Divine, as I also believe that there should be no supplemental death penalty, attached to any guilty verdict of life without parole. This inmate should forge ahead with his petitions and pleas since he finds himself in a very precarious situation. I understand that some of my readers will feel as though we need not concern ourselves with a murderer. We should throw away the proverbial key and forget about his existence, however, since His Son declared that He will pardon all sins through a repentant heart, we may at least try to comprehend the unconditional love and forgiveness, that His Son feels for this transgressor. What will become of his relatively short-lived existence? I understand that we do not know which day we shall expire; however, this prisoner is cognizant of how close his death truly is, as he reflects upon the final injection, from which he will die. Let us all think of our own death as impending or approaching quickly, for we know not when our own expiration will take place. Let us, therefore, apologize to His Son, since we have said many hurtful words, and have acted on some offensive ideas, as these behaviors have placed others in distress during the improper situations, we have created. Let us also ask for forgiveness from our Higher Power, in concert with our apology to Jesus, since we live for today, and only have the present, as no other unit of time, has been promised to us. Since this inmate has traveled a sinful road, he may intuitively commence praying on his own, as he attempts to cling to our God, in order to receive some inner peace. Communicating with our Higher Power on an elementary level, would be most significant, as the inmate's desire to converse with Him, may have been implanted in his mind by our Higher Power. This inmate may recapture his beliefs, by recollecting and humbly reciting just a simple prayer. I completely have faith, that a fresh and healthy relationship can begin between our Heavenly Father and the inmate, as long as he desperately begins to seek out our Higher Power's attention through his communion with God. Killing is against what Jesus taught us, even though, in the Old Testament it states that, "...you shall give life for life, eye for eye, tooth for tooth, hand for hand, foot for foot, burn for burn, wound for wound, stripe for stripe," as it is written. You can find these words in several locations throughout the Scripture, although, it is first stated in Exodus. As we know, Exodus is part of the Old Testament and presently we live life in the New Faith, as it is no longer, "...life for life, eye for eye..." since the new order states that we must, "...offer no resistance to injury. When a person strikes you on the right cheek, turn and offer him the other," as it is written. This quote does not only signify that we must physically be hurt, since we can also emotionally be harmed. Therefore, let us "turn the other cheek" and terminate the eventual fate, which this death row inmate is facing, as his execution is certainly not the correct answer, through the eyes of Jesus. We live and are alive, due to His Son's promises, and we, as a society of governmental laws, should not put this murderer to death. A fair share of these inmates remains mentally ill, as they do not receive their medications outside of prison; usually because they cannot afford them. If this inmate wishes to be vindicated, His Son is prepared to hear him repent with sincerity, and when His Son is certain of this inmate's full disclosure and confession, I firmly believe, that he shall be forgiven through the act of the crucifixion. This can only take place if the inmate remains alive long enough to prepare for his confession to our Lord. Let us pray for the people affected by both sides of this tragedy; the family of the person who was tragically killed, and the killer, as he begins to have faith in our Higher Power and His Son, as he may eventually become "an example" to all other inmates.

Chapter 35: Meditation and Prayer

Prayers take place in our souls, as well as in our minds. As it is written, "Dismiss all anxiety from your minds. Present your needs to God in every form of prayer and petitions full of gratitude. Then God's own peace, which is beyond all understanding, will stand guard over your hearts and minds, in Christ Jesus." God is ready to grant us peace in our lives, therefore, let us thank Him in prayer, for the gift He wishes to give us, through The Holy Spirit. At certain times, our minds can become cluttered and overwhelmed, since the various daily agendas we attend to, can be perplexing and unmanageable. This is an example of when prayer with our Higher Power becomes essential and urgent. Presently, what matters most significantly in our lives, are the communications and relationships we experience with our Higher Power and His Son, as we plan to follow their guidance, by executing the appropriate actions, which are mentioned in these communications. When we are inclined to feel frazzled and anxious, let us flip through the pages of the spiritual text, upon which our own religion is based. I primarily visit the Christian Bible, however, there are numerous texts, such as the: Torah, Quran, Egyptian Book of the Dead, Tao Te Ching and the Sutras which can all become useful tools, since these texts will void the worries of this world away, and allow our Higher Power to rescue us, as we continue to reflect upon our most inner and sobering thoughts. Our minds and souls are spiritually connected to each other, as His declarations enter our souls first-of-all. Next, our intuition is formed, and then this intuition becomes a complete puzzle of visions and emotions, which is then, dissected into words of wisdom by our mind, which finally helps us to wash our weariness away. We should begin to feel some well-earned relief, by using our intuition and our mind, as they help us to figure out the difficult predicaments our world presents to us. Reciting rote prayers, over and over again like a mantra, can also become a form of healing meditation, as we tap into our peaceful places of existence. Our mantra can also assist those of us who suffer from an increase in: heart rate, and/or blood pressure, and/or quick shallow breaths. Our meditational prayer is able to decrease these specific biorhythms, just as a traditional meditation would perform. Our bodies will begin to relax and heal themselves. Personally, I do not make any sound while I meditate, since I enjoy the quietness of my surroundings. This helps me to use my mind, in order to lift my consciousness up and onto a higher plateau, where the rest of the world melts away, and all that remains in our mind is our complete focus upon the three Entities. I also enjoy expressing the 'Hail Mary' and the 'Act of Contrition' as meditational prayers. Subsequent to our meditational prayers, we should anticipate to be freed from the anxieties of this world, as we continue to deeply reflect upon each wonder, which our Higher Power has created for each of us, as He is our greatest source of well-being. At times I play a tranquil CD of wind instruments at a low volume, which gives off sounds of a primal environment. This helps me to clear my head of all insignificant debris, as I am able to transfer this gentleness, from the workings of my mind at home, into the daily routine of unavoidable activities and challenges at work, as I am now able to calmly enter my day, with a profound inner peace, and a source of satisfaction.

Chapter 36: Through God's Point of View

Many times, we simply exist alone with our own thoughts, and continue to reflect upon every one of these thoughts, from our own point of view. Let us turn away from our tunnel vision, as we may instead be open to inspect matters from our Higher Power's point of view, since this can only improve our relationship with Him. We will understand Him better, if we begin to interpret the history of the human race and its Creator, as we cautiously delve into how He may truly feel about all of us. As we recall in the beginning, He created humanity, as His unabated love for us was apparent, since He gave us this beautiful, new world. He simply asked us to adhere to His desires, which were for our own good. He became unfortunately frustrated with Adam and Eve, due to their rejection of His wishes. Our sinful nature became most apparent to Him, when the prince of darkness enticed Adam and Eve to sin, since they managed to do the opposite of what God had asked of them. Adam and Eve, as well as their descendants, perpetrated many transgressions; no matter how small nor how big the iniquity, since these sins frequently continued to upset our Higher Power, due to the constant need for humanity's flesh-driven gratification. He understood that everyone continued to sin without regret, and everyone needed to be brought to justice for their transgressions, as He grew tired of their impurity and defilement. As a result of these sins, God became angry and disappointed with us, as He promptly acted as our disciplinarian, when He was not content with our behavior. As it is written, "When the Lord saw how great was man's wickedness on earth, and how no desire that his heart conceived was ever anything but evil, he regretted that he had made man on earth, and his heart was grieved. So, the Lord said: 'I will wipe out from the earth the men whom I have created, and not only the men, but also the beasts and the creeping things and the birds of the air, for I am sorry that I made them.'" Even though our Higher Power continuously watched over us, we still managed to commit sin after sin. We must surely believe that we regretfully failed at fulfilling His expectations, by inappropriately responding to His desires. Sadly, we have conducted ourselves similar to spoiled children, by eating fruit from the tree of knowledge, and by all of us continuing to act sinfully. Our Higher Power must have wondered why He had wasted His efforts in creating a soul for each of us, since He may have thought that these souls would keep us from committing, so many sins. The beauty of our soul is that it can help us to be penitent, faithful to God, and loving towards our neighbors; only if we ask for this help, however, we have acted evil and spoiled, as we continue to dismiss His intentions and rely upon our frailties, which causes us to execute too many sins, on a daily basis. It is as if He has encountered the actions and reactions of some two-year-old's, except that we are in the external form of fully-grown adults. Living for our flesh instead of for our Higher Power's wishes, we continue to find it difficult to obey our Creator. We will invariably remain His children, even though He sees us act as overindulged juveniles, as we pout or even become angry in certain situations, since we do not place our attention on anyone or anything else, but our own proclivity and toxic ambitions. As it is written, "What comparison can I use for the men of today? What are they like? They are like children squatting in the city squares and calling to their playmates, 'We piped you a tune but you did not dance, we sang you a dirge but you did not wail.'" Let us try to surrender ourselves and ask for our Heavenly Father's guidance, especially since we understand that this would be the easier, and the more peaceful way to live. The emotional bags of cement that we carry upon our shoulders, would finally be given to and lifted by Jesus, as we would begin to sense our relaxation, and our great love for His Son. Since our Higher Power loves us so much, He devised a solution for our sinful human nature, as He sent His only Son down to earth in order to die for the afterlife of our souls. His Son died upon the cross so that we could be gifted a new life, as Jesus was now endowed with the ability to absolve us from our sins. The new message from above was filled with love, and an abiding faith, as our Higher Power saw that this was good. This solution allowed Him to maintain an unconditional, and an unimaginable love for all of us, as our Savior promised us a grace-filled afterlife, if we invoke His name when we repent for our sins. This one exceptional action, performed by Jesus Christ, saved all of humanity, as we now have the ability to remain close to Him and to His Father, in the afterlife. Our Savior's unconditional love, bountiful mercy, and genuine forgiveness, are tremendously important gifts that Jesus gives us of Himself. I believe that the reason that His Son is boundlessly merciful with us, is partially due to the experience which He shared with us, as He lived as a human for thirty-three years on earth. Jesus encountered all of the same temptations that we struggle with, in addition to other enticements which are portrayed in Scripture. While His Son lived upon the earth, our Higher Power's elevated frustration level with us, seemed to decrease immeasurably, even though His love for us remained identical through both the Old and the New Testaments. Let us recognize that His Son was our Higher Power's greatest gift to us. Even though we have a strong bond and perhaps a slightly difficult past with Him, we shall always love our Heavenly Father, for the great sacrifice He has made for all of us.

Chapter 37: Lying

Do you consider yourself to be a deceptive person? We become liars soon after we learn how to speak, and each of our lies are formulated by our own design, as we quickly learn that we can use these lies to our advantage. We learn that by imagining and recounting certain intriguing information about our existence, our reality starts to blur and bend within our own minds, as our lives become full of lies. Perhaps our lives are boring, or we envy the way someone else lives, and therefore, we continue to pull a veil over ourselves, while we tell others certain implausible stories, which help us seem superior and interesting in comparison to our true existence. Our lies may resonate through a friend's heart as words of honesty, however, our friend may learn subsequently, that we had lied to him, as these creative words simply become disappointing and embarrassing. Our good reputation has now become sullied, as we are now labelled as a liar. Every time we express ourselves and deceive someone else, our Higher Power becomes heartily disappointed in us. We spew falsehoods, as our attention seeking behavior continues to pursue a reaction, by the other individual. Some liars tend to believe that they merely bend the truth, however, in all reality, the liar becomes engrossed in a depraved fantasy world. As it is written, the Son says, "Why do you not understand what I say? It is because you cannot bear to hear my word? The father you spring from is the devil, and willingly you carry out his wishes. He brought death to man from the beginning, and has never based himself within the truth; the truth is not in him. Lying speech is his native tongue; he is a liar and the father of lies." As it is written, "Never let evil talk pass your lips; say only the good things men need to hear, things that will really help them." These two Bible quotes verify that lying is a dangerous practice, as we must never pursue the devil's precepts. Let us recall that His Son is the Truth, and lights our passageway to a fulfilling spiritual life, as lying darkens this possibility. Lying may seem as if it is an insignificant sin, however, this is far from the truth. When we use our voices in order to deceive, we understand, that, even though we are not using an instrument of pain in order to wound others, we are cognizant that our lies have the capability of cutting one another's emotions and sensitivities quite deeply. At a certain time, we may want to apologize to the person we have deceived, in order to repair the confidence which was broken. Let this apology take place for the good of the other person, and for the good of our own soul. Let us also apologize to His Son. At various times, I do lie, primarily since I do not wish to hurt another individual's feelings, however, the reality of the situation is that my falsification remains a non-truth, which functions against His Word. I am reminded that Judas of Iscariot lied to the 'Lamb of God' at the Last Supper, when he deceived Jesus and turned Him over to the executioners in return for thirty pieces of silver. At the Last Supper, [which His Son also called the Passover meal, since the significance of both Passover meals memorialize the freedom gained from a type of bondage; either sin or slavery] the Son declared, "I assure you one of you is about to betray me. Distressed at this, they began to say to him one after another, 'surely it is not I Lord?'" He replied: "The man who has dipped his hand into the dish with me is the one who will hand me over. The Son of Man is departing, as Scripture says of him, but woe to that man by whom the Son of Man is betrayed. Better for him if he had never been born," as it is written. Effectuating a deception or a betrayal, by adding false information to the essence of a story is also not living within the boundaries of reality. Let us refuse to lie anymore, so that we will experience a profound and penetrating innocence and freedom. Also, let us leave the truthful story or truthful response in the quietude of the moment, when it is the other person's turn to speak, since we should not be burdened with having to stimulate the other person's emotions. By feeling a responsibility for entertaining the other person, we may execute a lie by: unnecessarily adding more words onto a true statement in order to make a fascinating story, communicating what is easiest at the moment, or attempting not to injure another person's sensitivities. These are never satisfactory reasons to lie. Our only goal here is to declare the authentic and factual nature of our speech, and therefore, I humbly believe that it is meant for us to arrive at this conclusory statement: ultimate honesty with others and ourselves is important for our mental health and for our Higher Power's contentment.

Chapter 38: Hasty Agenda

We tend to rush through our lives with unrelenting urgency, as we have simply become unable to focus on one task at a time anymore. We have become accustomed to wielding various tasks at the same time, since our lives have become busier than ever before. We are proud to wear this as a badge of honor, which we now label as 'multi-tasking.' This unnecessary hastiness speaks to many of us, since we have started developing a poor medical profile, due to the amount of stress we carry upon our shoulders. Therefore, we have now required ourselves to significantly change from our harried practices, into a less stressful and more peaceful routine. This will occur when we accept our Higher Power and His Son as our mentors, as we should deliver our stress onto their shoulders, and only then, will we desire to carve-out a few time slots during the day, in order to spend some time with ourselves and our mentors. Decluttering our schedules will certainly be a challenge, however, if we keep our focus on our communion with the Entities, then we will have the capability to maintain a simple existence, in what has become a complex society. Even as others continue to demand some of our precious time, we can begin to clear an insignificant amount of time from our schedules, as we surprisingly find ourselves with less pressure on our shoulders, and less to do on a daily basis, as one of these insignificant amounts of time, begin to add onto other insignificant amounts of time, which finally forms a significant block of time. We become comforted and contented, as we discover a very important 'little chunk of time,' for which we will develop some quiet moments for ourselves. Personally, my daily schedule was invariably brimming with details I needed to attend to, or thought I needed to attend to, and as a result, I caught myself cutting into my friend's conversation with my own sentiments, as I began to speak hurriedly, on top of her sentiments. I never allowed my friend to speak, since I falsely knew that my part of the discussion, needed to be heard immediately, as I was desperate and found it necessary to fast-forward my thoughts and emotions to her. I thought that if my friend heard my ideas first, then she would understand the correctness of my thinking. I sensed the emptiness and loneliness inside of myself, since I knew that conversing at the very same time was indeed rude and inappropriate. I also echoed my friend's sentiments while she spoke, however, I did not mean this in a discourteous manner; I must attempt to terminate this troublesome habit. Finally, becoming weary and demoralized, as I spoke on top of everyone I conferred with, I was determined to truly listen to what information people were willing to share with me. In place of ignoring them, or thinking about what I was going to say next, I remained quiet, and ingested the knowledge from the conversation. Carefully listening to what others disclosed to me, made such a positive difference in my life, and in the lives of others. People have the need to be heard and validated, and therefore, let us extend that courtesy to them, especially since we have worked on freshly decluttering our lives. When we reach a point of silence in the conversation, only one of us should start to speak again. This is how we must successfully share our thoughts and emotions, as we create an atmosphere of relaxation and peace, instead of a place of contention. Therefore, let us not run, but triumphantly decelerate the pace of our lives, by removing unimportant matters from our schedules, as we learn to comfortably walk through life, so that we have more time for ourselves, and time to communicate with the Entities of the Complete Being. We must learn to confer with others in a more engaging and polite fashion, as we begin to assimilate, and hopefully retain the information that others will share with us. We will begin to feel much more fulfilled internally, as we become alive; simply by listening.

Chapter 39: Angels

As it is written, "These are they whom the Lord has sent to patrol the earth," as they answered the angel of the Lord who was standing among the myrtle trees and said, "We have patrolled the earth; see the whole earth is tranquil and at rest!" Also, as it is written, "To which of the angels has God ever said, 'Sit at my right hand till I make your enemies your footstool'? Are they not all ministering spirits, sent to serve those who are to inherit salvation?" Angels perform the actions of a protective friend, and were sent to serve those of us who live on earth, however, they will never resemble how significant Jesus' connection is with His Father, as Jesus possesses an indescribable intimacy with Him. Both of these relationships with our Higher Power are vastly different from one another. During the time of the Mosaic Covenant, the Israelites were fraught with great fear due to God's disappointment with them. Angels were known as ministers or intermediaries, as the Jewish people believed that if they prayed through these angels, our Higher Power would accept their pleas and wishes more easily. At times, angels came to the Israelites in their dreams. The most famous instance of this occurred, when the archangel Gabriel appeared to the Virgin Mary. This angel was sent to tell her that God had chosen her to bare His Son, who would be named Emmanuel, which means 'God with us.' Protective angels have a special calling; as it is written, "See, I am sending an angel before you, to guard you on the way and bring you to the place I have prepared." Each of our angels of protection, help to guide us closer to our Higher Power, and our eternal reward. I ask Jesus, as well as my angel of protection, to keep me aware of all malicious circumstances and beings, so that I will not fall into the hands of the dark force. It is up to us, if we remain close to our angels of protection, since they continue to remain in our soul; even now. Let us not forget them, as they may come to us in a dream, and perform the Lord's work. Personally, as I continue on my journey through life, I view my angel of protection as if it is a friend, who keeps me safe, and reminds me of spiritual matters which I can overlook. As we arise from sleep, our angels remind us to bless ourselves with the sign of the cross, and address our Higher Power, as we should express our gratitude to Him for granting us a new day. We should maintain at least a succinct conversation with our Higher Power, during this essential moment during the day. Any moment is essential, as long as it takes place in the present. Angels are Spirits, as one angel of protection is sent to each newborn, so that we are protected by them, from the very beginning. Angels are formed in Heaven, and most of them are instantly cloned from other angels, except for the special angels of protection which protect the Entities of the Complete Being. I humbly believe that the protection which our angels offer us, persists subsequent to our death; whether we enter Heaven or the temporary premises, prior to our entrance into Heaven. Some of the angels may either form part of our Higher Power's spiritual force, or have been tempted by the prince of darkness, as these angels also continue to have a free will; just as we do. Our Higher Power's special angel of protection had assisted in defending Him during a war of cataclysmic proportion, which occurred as the archangel Michael and his legion of good angels, fought against the evil dragon and his corrupt band of vicious angels. Good triumphed over evil, as our Higher Power, the archangel Michael, and His virtuous angels were completely victorious.

Chapter 40: Judgment

As it is written, "If you want to avoid judgment, stop passing judgment. Your verdict on others will be the verdict passed to you. The measure with which you measure another will be used to measure you." When we judge others, we are then judged with the same criteria and in the same manner, which we provide to others. Our judgment of others usually occurs instantaneously, however, it tends to vacate our consciousness rather slowly. As we begin to evaluate another person's appearance, or begin to gather a first impression, we often continue to inspect this person with tunnel vision, in which we only see evidence of ugliness and mischievousness, so that we may consider ourselves superior to them. It seems as though we expect more from others, than we do from ourselves. We might not wish to hurt another person's feelings; however, I believe that this person is capable of promptly noticing when we begin to judge them. At times, we even adjudicate the entire character of another person, which occurs when we should be reflecting upon ourselves, and our own inadequacies. As we delve into another person's behavior, we may begin to experience a distaste of his character. For example, he may exhibit some unpopular characteristics, such as boastfulness and jealousy. We know that we do not have the ability to alter his behavior, however, we do have the capability to change our own behavior, and the way in which we view his behavior. Let us, therefore, completely concentrate upon our transgressions, so that when we pray to our Savior and are within His presence, He will absolve us of our own iniquities. We tend to see others from a rather narrow point of view, as our appraisal of others is almost always non-forgiving, which informs us that our judgment of others remains inconsiderate, inadequate, and non-welcoming. Our assessment should be terminated immediately, if we want the Divine to absolve us of this particular sin. As we focus intently upon our judgment of others, we should declare, 'cancel, cancel' in our minds, so that we may impede our present thinking pattern, and alter its course towards a new orientation. Personally, I believe that the origin of these evaluations, egress from the dark force, and in order to counteract this sin, let us think of at least one or two positive attributes about the person, who we have just finished adjudicating in our mind. Over time, our intrinsic decisions concerning others will become tedious, as we will hopefully decide to discontinue this noticeable sin, and slaughter our condemnatory dragon, which appears every time we judge others. When we are judged by Jesus, our intention is to be judged as minimally as possible, since His Covenant with us says that we should not attempt to judge others. As it is written, "The Father himself judges no one, but has assigned all judgment to the Son, so that all men may honor the Son just as they honor the Father. He who refuses to honor the Son refuses to honor the Father who sent him." I believe that the Entity who created us, should be the only one who should judge us, however, in our case, this responsibility was given to another Entity, as our Heavenly Father willingly passed this duty onto His Son. As mercy and love emanate from His heart, Jesus will be the final judge; not only of our soul and its iniquities, however, He will also judge us on the strength of our faith, and the merit of our actions.

Chapter 41: Care Giver

At a certain time in our life, we may become responsible for another life. We may begin to care for, and be deliberate with either a mentally challenged child, or a parent. This can be an overwhelming responsibility, as we begin to realize, that our lives will never be the same. Even though we have accepted this responsibility into our world, it remains necessary for our Higher Power to consistently exist and linger within our mind, since we will require His assistance, just as our family member will require our assistance. We have become painfully aware that our relative will not make much cognitive progress, even though we have accepted the moral obligation of helping our beloved family member daily. In all probability, our family member will not make any further intellectual progress, while in our capable hands; no matter how much time elapses. Occasionally, we have secured help in the form of a nurse's aide, or a social worker, as these people are generously sent to us by the city government in order to ameliorate our situation, although this aid does not remain with us for long periods of time. We find that we do not have the ability, nor the desire to pay attention to our own wants and needs. Our family member seems to require that we be with him during his every waking moment, which creates an emotional energy called stress. As we slide into the caboose of life, he lives his life in the conductor's compartment inside of our imaginary train, as our mind informs us that he is in control, since we must take care of all of his needs, prior to our own. Being at peace with our loved one, is not an easy path to master, however, we have begun to understand the difficulties that our relative experiences, as we also recognize that life itself is completely dependent upon our perseverance. As it is written, "In him who is the source of my strength I have strength for everything." Let us, therefore, take solace from our Higher Power, as it is necessary to hold Him in our hearts and in our minds, since we need His energy and His strength to care of our beloved family member. Another affirmation which may also be beneficial to us is the Serenity Prayer: 'God grant me the serenity to accept the things I cannot change, the courage to change the things I can, and the wisdom to know the difference.' By exerting much of our time with our mentally-challenged loved one, we become painfully aware that we cannot find enough time to communicate with the Entities of the Complete Being. Even though our consciousness may be overburdened with our relative's needs, we must understand that our actions, which continuously support our family member, are prayers unto themselves. These prayers are sent to our Higher Power for our intentions, which include the grace we need to care for our family member, who continues to struggle with life. We may start to feel some serenity, since our assistance is helping his cause, and therefore, similar to osmosis, our serenity will be passed onto our beloved family member, each time we feel peace flow into our own lives. Even though we respond to our family member's every whim, our devotion to him becomes unabated, as he continues to remain dependent upon us, except for when he lays down and sleeps. We are vigilant, solicitous and observant, as we connect ourselves with our family member, even to a greater extent as time progresses. As it is written, "Your love must be sincere. Detest what is evil, cling to what is good. Love one another with the affection of brothers. Anticipate each other in showing respect. Do not grow slack but be fervent in spirit; he whom you serve is the Lord." Our Lord is within my relative.

Chapter 42: Fate/Destiny

Fate means that an action, which has already taken place, was once previously prophesized to do so; such as the birth of Jesus, as this is an action, that has already taken place in the New Testament, and was once previously prophesized to do so in the Old Testament. This action will inevitably occur; and whatever we did, through the course of time between, when the action had been previously prophesized, and when the action actually occurred, cannot have been altered by us, in any way. It is all part of fate. Although we remain in control of our own lives, we should comprehend that He already knows what our choices will be, even though we have not yet formed them. Let us understand that each of us has a free will, as this liberty has been granted to us by our Higher Power, so that we can live as we see fit, which in our case, takes place in a spiritual reality. We continue to make our own decisions and perform our own actions, even though we will have previously asked Him for His guidance. Even though we make our own decisions, and have felt His guidance, all of the decisions in our lives are simply considered part of fate. It is not that our Higher Power has simply given each of us a role to be played on earth; and it is not that our Father in Heaven has structured a plan for each of our lives, which we must carry out; and certainly, we do not feel as though He has merely created puppets out of us, who must simply adhere to a scripted life. None of these examples would be considered fate. We do not have the capability of truly comprehending how our planet will appear, when Jesus Christ comes to earth for the second time. Let us not worry about the demise of our planet, since it is destined to happen anyway, as it is written in Revelation that our world will become decimated by fire, and shall be incompatible with our existence. As it is written, "The consummation of all is close at hand. Therefore, do not be perturbed; remain calm so that you will be able to pray. Above all, let your love for one another be constant, for love covers a multitude of sins." Since our Higher Power has given me a choice to make, regarding how I should live my life, I chose to go to college instead of working. Our mind and my mother had previously been cognizant of this decision since I had enjoyed high school all four years. All of my actions, which take place prior to making my final decision on which course of action to take, cannot have been altered in any way. This is fate. Therefore, everything that we do, is destined to take place; even if we pray to our Higher Power, in order to help us change our course of action, these prayers and the alteration of our course of action were also destined to take place. Let us recall that our Higher Power is a quantum of energy, who travels in and around us, as He keeps His 'finger on the pulse' of His greatest creation. God lives in the present, so that He can assist us by creating real differences in our lives, as we ask Him for His guidance. Does the present realm mean now, or maybe within a couple of minutes? I humbly believe that the present realm signifies that God experiences everything with all of us right now, within the present, and since He does not adhere to any time constraints, He must have always existed, and will continue to eternally exist. We are not capable of estimating how old our Higher Power could be, since segmented measurements of duration do not exist in His world, as they do in our world. He, therefore, never lives within, nor directly experiences the past or the future, although He is cognizant of what occurs in both our pasts and our futures. The three realms become an open book, as He is able to recall the past, experience the present with us, and is completely cognizant of the future; all at once. God is omnipotent, and it is for this reason that fate must exist. The fate that exists, makes us aware that He can see the final outcome of our actions. I humbly believe that, all situations, and resolutions to these situations, were destined to happen. For example, our Higher Power promised us, in the Old Testament, that His Son would one day be born amongst us, and in turn, our Higher Power would make Him a throne in Heaven, forevermore. We all know that this was destined to be, since it has become our reality. As it is written, God says, "And when your time comes and you rest with your ancestors, I will raise up your heir after you, sprung from your loins, and I will make his kingdom firm. It is he who shall build a house for my name. And I will make his royal throne firm forever. I will be a father to him, and he shall be a son to me..." This is fate, because it is promised to us in the Old Testament, but does not take place until the New Testament. The Old Testament validates some of what will occur in the New Testament, as the information in the Old Testament was destined to occur in the New Testament. Looking back at my life through a rear-view-mirror, it seems as though I have lived for such a brief period. As it is written, "You are a vapor that appears briefly and vanishes." Our lives seem as though they exist only for a fraction of an instant, as it takes this amount of time to expire a breath of air, or for a raindrop to fall from the heavens, as it gently creates concentric circles moving across a pond. This raindrop appears to be indistinguishable from all other raindrops, however, it seems as though this particular raindrop has remained with us, just as long as our lives had once existed, as our essences continue to aptly be delivered from this planet. We only exist on earth for what is comparatively a nano-second in time, speaking in relative terms, since the creation of our planet arrived several billion years ago, and we as humans only exist for what is a mere several decades. We find it necessary, yet difficult to follow His Son's interests, instead of pursuing our own never-ending desires, which are the desires of the flesh, and the desires of the dark force. Temptations continually trouble us, and therefore the Scripture reveals that, "Everyone is busy seeking his own interests rather than those of Jesus Christ" as it is written. Even though some people drift randomly through life, continuously looking for objects or situations that will please them externally, our sole source of contentment and satisfaction presents itself with our Lord, internally. Let us awaken within the Son's gentle spirit, in which we arise and become enveloped in mercy and unconditional love. His Son's task of judging our words and works maintains its genuine importance, since we continue to live with a free will, as we are 100% responsible for our every action, even if we have asked God to guide us. We are liable for the status and condition of our own soul, since we remain accountable for our choices. Our soul will continue to remain alive for eternity, when we shed our expired flesh and free our glistening jewel.

Chapter 43: Construction or Destruction

We remain exclusively responsible for the construction and destruction of our own lives. We maintain this responsibility through the thoughts we reflect upon, and through the culmination of our actions that follow. We become accountable to His Son for the judgments we make, as well as the behaviors we execute, which are born from these thoughts. We continue to be liable for our own resolutions and self-possessed conclusions, even if we have asked Him to assist us in taking control of our daily lives, so that we may become unburdened and more at peace. If we give ourselves over to His Son, and allow His intentions to regulate our lives, effectuating more construction than destruction, and an easier and more fulfilling life, we continue to be responsible for our actions, even if we remain sinners, since every activity we perform, must pass through our own thought processes, prior to the execution of our conduct. Also, let us remember that we may still ask Him for various items or circumstances that we wish for, even though we have turned the command of our lives over to Him. What exactly does turn the command of our lives over to Him actually mean? It does not mean that He will control us, however, it does signify that He will send messages to our intuition, which will ultimately be delivered to our minds. These messages offer His guidance, so that we will not be tempted to sin, as He will reveal a novel idea and another direction for us to take, in order to inhibit us from perpetrating more sins. This signifies that we will go about our lives in a much more relaxed state, since we can now act with patience and ease, as we listen to our intuition. We are ready to take this step forward, since our lives have been so chaotic, when we attempt to remain in control. We worry too much about our worldly existence, as we surely need some relief from this state of being. This will also give us the chance to be in constant contact with His Son, by asking Him to assist us daily, as He guides us towards a pathway to serenity. This signifies that our actions will be more constructive, as we abide by His intentions, and live our life according to

His Son's promises to us. Let us follow His Son, as He wants our life to be full of genuine contentment and peacefulness, as He offers us a conclusion to our mental anguish. This ease and peacefulness I speak of, will relieve us, as we exclude ourselves from the excessive worries and indulgences, concerning worldly matters. I believe, that we ultimately understand how we shall present this burden of control over to Him, as we should simply ask this of His Son in our prayers, so that we may begin to feel delight, joy, and freedom. As it is written, "Take my yoke upon your shoulders and learn from me, for I am gentle and humble of heart. Your souls will find rest, for my yoke is easy and my burden light." I am aware that a number of our brave veterans, arrive home with amputated limbs. Some of these veterans have accepted their situations with prayer, resolve, and optimism. Since His Son should be at the helm of our existence, let our veterans heed this message and successfully re-enter society, while adopting a new set of circumstances from His Son, as they begin living life to the fullest once again. Many of us are aware of post-traumatic stress disorder, as these soldiers struggle with a heavy heart, when they arrive home; I am not addressing these particular veterans until the last part of this chapter. I am, however, speaking about my friend, who knows a remarkable young woman. This veteran lives with an amputation of the left lower leg, as she was in Afghanistan fighting for her life, and the lives of all Americans, when a bomb suddenly went off. She has always been a positive soul, and therefore, when she received her prosthesis, she began taking baby steps with it immediately. Some months later, she proceeded to jog on the treadmill, and then subsequently started running outside. She is truly an inspiration to all of us, since she accepted an unfortunate circumstance, and created something positive. She even competed in a triathlon. On the day of the race, her spirit soared with confidence, as she was ready to win. When the race was over, she had not placed in the top three positions, however, she had finished the course by posting one of her best times; she was genuinely proud of herself. Let us deliver ourselves over to His Son and our Higher Power daily, and receive our individual lives with patience and appreciation. Of course, living with post-traumatic stress disorder is totally exhausting, since it is a mental condition, over which the veterans have little control. I have had some experience with our veterans who have PTSD, and they cannot just jump back into their lives at will, after their tour of duty. Veterans, please find some contentment and attempt to find some peace. We all thank-you for your service, as we continue to pray for you.

Chapter 44: Unguarded Words

As it is written, "Sin will no longer have power over you; you are now under grace, not under the law. Just because we are not under the law but under grace, are we free to sin? By no means!" As this quote affirms, we now possess the privilege of requesting His Son's compassion and mercy, which He uses to absolve us from the sins we have committed, however, just because we live in His grace, does not indicate that we are free to sin. Let us never take advantage of the absolution He had promised to us, since we may understand how easily we could be forgiven, just by simply asking for His mercy, even though we are undeniably non-repentant for the sin we had perpetrated. Due to the painful manner in which He suffered for us on the cross, we should feel a profound sadness within ourselves, as we endeavor to comprehend the full gravity of His death. This awareness will hopefully cause us to remain without sin, for a substantial period of time. As it is written, "I assure you, on judgment day people will be held accountable for every unguarded word they speak. By your words you will be acquitted, and by your words you will be condemned." The word unguarded here translates into the term thoughtless, which is further translated into the words: inconsiderate and deceptive. If we become thoughtless, and begin to disclose a few lies while texting or speaking into our electronic devices, then we will be obliged to answer for these imprudent uses of language, either now, when we ask for His forgiveness, or immediately subsequent to our demise, when we first meet His Son, and all of us are transferred into the temporary premises. There are too many illustrations of these unguarded words to count, however, if we remain cognizant and alert enough to request Jesus' forgiveness for these deceptive words, we shall be released from encountering His Son's judgment, for the thoughtless words which we have spoken. Let us be aware of what we say, what we text, or what we write, since we should not want to: debase one another, lie to one another, or shout obscenities towards one another. Waiting in prayer, prior to His death upon the cross, we remember that Jesus communicated an emotional plea to His Father while He remained in the garden. His Son must have wondered why His death needed to conclude in such a vile, and brutal way, however, His Son's faith in His Father is unparalleled, and therefore, He need not question His Father a second time regarding His demise. The Holy Spirit bestows the gift of forgiveness to each of us, so that we may have the ability to forgive one another, as we may continue to live through His Son, who built His ministry upon: mercy, compassion, forgiveness, and most important of all, faith. As it is written, "For we hold that a man is justified by faith apart from the observance of the law. Are we then abolishing the law by means of faith? Not at all! On the contrary, we are confirming the law." The New Testament fulfills the Old Testament, by acting upon the lessons, which the Old Testament had previously taught us. The Old Testament validates the importance of what the New Testament declares, as certain prophets and our Higher Power reveal His Son's birth to us, which was destined to happen, as His Son later became the central figure within the New Testament. Let us learn how to speak and act without sin, as we shall attend to both the Father and His Son's advice, as they ask us to keep watch on all of the unguarded and inadvertent words we utter. We are indeed fortuitous to live in this era, since the New Testament has already been recorded, and is available to us whenever we wish to read it.

Chapter 45: Sacred Mysteries

The enlightenment which pours forth from the Lord, and develops within our souls before traveling to our minds, inspires our essence by helping us to understand important clues, to several of the Sacred Mysteries. The Sacred Mysteries are puzzles, some of which concern: His existence, His purpose for us, His Kingdom in Heaven, and many more secrets which continue to tease our intellect, and unfortunately, will not be thoroughly explained to us here on earth, even though we simply have the desire to understand everything associated with our Higher Power, and everything spiritual that connects to our own lives. For instance, one of the Sacred Mysteries asks us to ponder the question, 'Where is Heaven, and how will we feel once we are there?' We all know that He does not wish to disclose the answers to any of the Sacred Mysteries, until our souls have departed to an afterlife. We cannot fully appreciate the answer to the question, since we must simply feel Heaven for ourselves. The entire reason that He will not declare the explanations to all of these Mysteries, comes about because our curiosity creates an abundance of interest in Him and in His Kingdom, which is one of the methods He uses to sustain our attention, our fascination, and our genuine faith in Him, as we will never be truly satisfied as long as we remain on earth, which is where He refuses to grant us more than just a few pieces of each of these spiritual puzzles. Another Sacred Mystery invites another secret; one of which concerns an enigma called eternity. Personally, I do not believe that we currently have enough reasoning capacity to truly understand the concept of eternity, however, we would be most grateful for the response to this conundrum, and the mind in order to perceive the explanation to this concept. Unfortunately, this disclosure does not happen to be within our grasp, or within our reality, just now. I believe that when we enter an afterlife, our search for intimacy and knowledge of the Complete Being, will be fulfilled. He has frequently explained to us, that He will gift us with genuine love, hope, and faith, if we live a simple, yet considerable life in prayer, however, I fathom that most of us wish to appreciate the brilliance of God through the Sacred Mysteries. Even though we are unable to see Him with our own eyes, we see Him through the good works of others, and hear Him through our conversational prayers; not through His voice, but through our intuition. The information we acquire regarding His intentions, and possibly a few of His Sacred Mysteries, are purely contingent upon our reception of His Word: through the narrations of His Son, through His own spoken Words, and through the execution of His actions, all which grace the pages of our Bibles. As it is written, "Whoever has seen me has seen the Father... Do you not believe that I am in the Father and the Father is in me? As it is written, "You yourselves will not be the speakers; the Spirit of your Father will be speaking in you;" these two quotes are an offer of proof, for the Father, the Son, and the Father's Spirit, which is The Holy Spirit, as they exist as the Complete Being, since all three Entities work as a whole, and become one Entity. As it is written, "Before the mountains were begotten and the earth and the world were brought forth, from everlasting to everlasting you are God." I wonder if the word "everlasting," could be perceived as a time frame other than eternity? This unit of time could signify that our Higher Power had existed within the heavens, perhaps for trillions of years, which in our mind is close to eternity, however, not necessarily an eternity, which is what we as Christians were taught to believe. Could our Higher Power have been created by another Source or Entity, trillions of years ago? If this is true, then who is the Entity who brought forth our Higher Power into His existence? Since there is absolutely no evidence which sustains this hypothesis in the Bible, I have concluded that our Higher Power has always existed and will continue to exist, as there is no other Entity, prior to or subsequent to God, Himself. Unfortunately, He will probably never reveal Himself to us in total. As it is written, "...and no one knows who the Son is except the Father, or who the Father is except the Son and anyone else to whom the Son chooses to reveal him." Total belief without total knowledge is admirable, as we are asked to have absolute faith, without the pieces of the puzzle that would fulfill our knowledge of our Higher Power, and the Complete Being. If our Higher Power does not limit us in certain ways, by amplifying our curiosity, while restricting certain information from us, then He knows that we will not continue to search for Him, since we, and our sinfully-driven flesh, will knowingly develop an undesirably indifferent attitude towards God and His Word. We may even remove our attention from our spirituality, and allow the desires of this world to have a greater effect on us. There are some of us who truly listen to the Father, at all times. We should try to imitate the lives of these people, who presently include our mentors, and the individuals who listened to God in the Bible, since He is pleased with their effort. As it is written, "Consider the case of Abraham: he believed God, and it was credited to him as justice. This means that those who believe are sons of Abraham. Scripture saw in advance that God's way of justifying the Gentiles would be through faith, as it foretold this good news to Abraham: 'All nations shall be blessed in you.' Thus it is that all who believe are blessed along with Abraham, the man of faith." As mankind attempts to resolve the Sacred Mysteries, let us not take-up too much of our time in doing so, as I am sure that these are meant to be uncompromisingly unsolvable, although I do fathom that we must continue to seek Him and His Kingdom, before all else.

Chapter 46: Anxiety

As I was taking a walk, I happened to reflect upon an illness I developed a few years ago, and how God helped me to mature, while dealing with this affliction. A few years back, I attempted to function the way I always had, even though I began to wrestle with a cruel illness, called anxiety. Whether we contract or develop an illness from birth, this may become one of our most desperate of times. We find ourselves speaking to our Higher Power with remarkable frequency, as we persist in asking Him to remove this ailment from our bodies or our minds. Even though we are suffering, our Higher Power is content and appreciative in one sense, since He enjoys the recurrent conversations, we have with Him. These dialogues we have with our Higher Power lead us to develop a most important relationship with Him. A number of people are plagued with various degrees of anxiety, as this disruptive illness may at times lead to uncontrollable panic attacks. During our anxious moments, we must sometimes make decisions of significant proportions, which will translate mental mistakes into action errors. I humbly believe that our anxiety, is caused or worsened by the dark force, since our innate ability to act and speak in the same manner, prior to our illness, was completely stripped away. This illness can prevent us from performing a job, solving a problem, or executing a simple task, as we become misled by the dark force. When we develop anxiety, we feel uncomfortable, nervous, and confused, especially when we must use our decision-making capacity, as our confidence has all of a sudden abandoned us, and we feel as though our confounded sense of consciousness, has fallen into the grip of someone or something else. At times, we do not act like ourselves, which is in part caused by the pent-up energy from our anxiety. Usually it disseminates as nervous energy or internal agitation, as we strongly dislike living as people, who are uncomfortable in their own skin. We continue to smile at others, so that our anxiety cannot easily be detected, even though we continue to feel extremely edgy. Our intellect used to properly regulate our thoughts, speech, and actions prior to the dawn of our anxiety, however, our illness causes us to emote, even though our minds are presently functioning with little control. Anxiety is looked upon as a weakness of the mind, and society's norm regarding this illness, informs us that if our minds were mentally stronger, then we should be capable of freeing ourselves from this suffocating sickness. Those of us who have suffered through anxiety, know that this statement is untrue, since our intellects are not weak. The mental effects stimulate behavioral outgrowths, which exhibit themselves for all to see. We have trouble solving life's various problems, as they are presented to us daily, and as a result, we become mentally and physically drained. Let us attempt to ultimately alter this uncertainty, while exchanging the doubt that is in our minds, with previously organized convictions which we possessed, prior to this unwelcomed sickness. Let the rest of us stop judging others so quickly, since they may be experiencing an illness they cannot control. We may easily take a pill, which has been prescribed for our anxiety, as the illness and the resulting consequences, may be postponed for a certain amount of time, however, the consequences return after the effects of the medication have concluded, a few hours later. Are we being fair to ourselves if we relinquish the chance to quiet our anxiety by different methods, other than acquiring a bit of chemical relief from a physician? We may have to suffer somewhat, since we made the decision to quell our own anxiety without the use of prescriptions, as we quiet our minds, by: listening to peaceful music, meditating, and conversing with our Higher Power. He will ultimately assist us, as long as we pray to Him for our relief. Let us look forward to the day in which our anxiety will leave our bodies and minds, as we continue to converse with our Higher Power and His Son. Let us pray for the stability of our confused minds, so that our anxiety will be remedied. As a result, we begin to freely and peacefully express ourselves to our Higher Power, as our conversational prayers will start to mend and steady our lives. There is no shame nor stigma in asking a physician for an anti-anxiety medication, which will assist us as it gives us a respite from our illness, especially if restoration through quietness and meditation fails us in the end.

Chapter 47: Healing the Sick

As I opened my Bible and began to read, I learned that Jesus had avoided healing a small number of debilitated people, who were from the fringes of society. It seemed that they had been awaiting His presence for a comforting cure of their painful ailments. We have come to know His Son as the most merciful of beings, however, there must be a reason why His miraculous powers did not affect this small group of individuals. His pattern of conduct, in this scenario, was contradictory and counterintuitive, since He usually helped to cure all others during similar circumstances. I humbly believe, that His Son had endeavored to relieve these few individuals of their disabilities, however, His miracle did not work, due to His Father's interference. Here, we see a difference between the Father, the authority figure within the Complete Being, and His Son. When His Son attempted to express His miraculous powers within this particularly small and disabled group, His Father was aware that these people had disrespected the Entities, far too many times for this group to be helped that day. They had no respect for His Son and no respect for life in general. It may have seemed to us, that His Son did not cure these few individuals, however, it was actually these few individual's selfish thoughts and their attention to worldly matters, which did not permit them to be healed. The people who were cured, had at least some faith in His Son, and had at least some love for the Complete Being. When we suffer from pain throughout our bodies, we naturally gravitate towards the One who can remove this agony from us, and if He listens to our continuous prayers and conversations, His Son may lessen or remove our misery. We will most likely, however unfortunately, terminate our successive and profound communication with Jesus, when we receive His relief of our affliction. We may decide to carelessly cast Him aside by not speaking to Him further, since we no longer need His Son's help for our sickness. Even though He was aware that He could not cure everyone, His Son also enjoyed speaking to the masses, mostly in parables, as He had a love of instructing them about: spirituality, His life, His Father's desires for us, and the Sacred History surrounding His own life, which are a few of the subjects and themes of the New Testament. Also documented in the New Testament are the familiar actions of a sickly man, who struggled through a dense crowd, to hopefully manage a glimpse of the Son, as he had absolute faith in His miraculous cures. He joyously discovered that by merely swiping His Son's garment, his ailment was then relieved. As it is written, "… The crowds scurried about the adjacent area and began to bring the sick on bedrolls to the place where they heard he was. Wherever he put in an appearance, in villages, in towns, or at crossroads, they laid the sick in the market places and begged him to let them touch just the tassel of his cloak. All who touched him got well." How do we generate the intense faith, which these people so beautifully exhibited and experienced, as they genuinely believed in Jesus, who came to cure them? We are capable of acquiring more belief in His Son, when we yearn for the passionate faith which we see others possess. This type of faith requires a positive mind-set and a complete knowledge, that our faith is sound and grounded in the conversations, we are so privileged to have with Him. Even though generating faith, through reading Scripture and praying, is distinct from completing our duties, these two distinct ideas remain related by the following quote; as it is written, "Be assured then, that faith without works is as dead as a body without breath." We must show the Complete Being that our faith is not empty, since we are prepared to help others who are in need, just as Jesus taught us. Another miracle, which His Son had completed, was the miracle in which Peter the apostle relinquished the safety of his boat, and began to walk on water. Subsequent to Jesus coaching him to walk on water, He executed this very same action along with Peter, however, as doubt began to creep into Peter's mind concerning what he continued to accomplish, his faith in the Son and himself began to diminish, as he eventually fell into the sea. As it is written, "Jesus at once stretched out his hand and caught him. 'How little faith you have!" he exclaimed. Why did you falter?'" "Once they had climbed into the boat, the wind died down. Those who were in the boat showed him reverence, declaring 'Beyond doubt you are the son of God!'"

Maintaining a true sense of faith in Jesus, casts out the uneasiness from our souls, and the dark force from our environment. Faith translates into: confidence, trust, loyalty, and hope. Simply put, we ought to affirm and support the necessity of a solemn request for more faith, when we begin to form our prayers for the day.

Chapter 48: Humility

Sometime during my elementary school years, my parents intimated that I should suppress my own needs and desires, and place them subsequent to the needs of others. Humility can be defined as the capability of focusing on, and taking care of another individual's needs before our own; possibly to our own detriment. My parents disclosed to me, that this behavior should not be executed, simply because they informed me of it; however, it should be performed, since humility is often stated in Scripture as something to which we should aspire. I find that humility produces a feeling of solicitude and benevolence, since caring for someone else's needs and desires, prior to our own, is considered as a gift, which has been given to another. Humility, offered with the best of our intentions, is not to be taken lightly, or taken advantage of in any way, since we wish to offer our consideration for others, completed with heartfelt emotions. With practice, the deference and respect we show to others, can become our reality. I believe that our Higher Power meant for us to feel spiritually fulfilled, when we had considered other people's wishes prior to our own, since giving of ourselves, prior to giving to ourselves is certainly admirable. Let us not confuse humility with weakness. He treasures when both parties feel genuinely good, as they both remain humble with each other, and work towards a symbiotic relationship. As a result, this signifies that I continue to look out for your interests before my own, and in turn, you look out for my interests first; however, if you do not look out for me prior to your own interests, you at least unintentionally, have looked out for the virtue of my soul, as I have been granted the chance to have been humble. As it is written, "Whoever exalts himself shall be humbled, but whoever humbles himself shall be exalted." As I read the Bible and other religious sources, I discovered that His Son maintained a posture of humility, when He came to serve us. When the Last Supper was taking place, His Son took a basin and towel, as He began washing and drying His disciple's feet; as it is written, "Do you understand what I just did for you? You address me as 'Teacher' and 'Lord,' and fittingly enough, for that is what I am. But if I washed your feet- I who am Teacher and Lord- then you must wash each other's feet. What I just did was to give you an example: as I have done, so you must do. I solemnly assure you, no slave is greater than his master; no messenger outranks the one who sent him. Once you know all these things, blest will you be if you put them into practice." When our Savior washed the feet of those who were His disciples, I understood this quote to signify that even though the master is greater than his slave, the master nevertheless washed and dried the feet of his slave, since the master refused to show his superiority over his slave, as he did not exalt himself by having his slave wash his feet. If we do not symbolically wash the feet of others, then we cannot accept His Son and His Covenant, nor can we accept our Higher Power, who had sent His Son. We should imitate His Son's humility, and we shall also seek what concerns His Son, as we should not engage in what may eventually entangle us within this world. Humility is not born-out of our world; however, it is a feature which is born-out of God's Kingdom. His Son has informed us of how we should act, so that we will either start, or continue to possess this understated posture and behavior. We should learn to act as Jesus did, as we should allow others' needs to be taken care of before our own needs, and hope to aid anyone we can, even when we are busy with our own circumstances. As it is written, "Never act out of rivalry or conceit; rather, let all parties think humbly of others as superior to themselves, each of you looking to other's interests rather than to his own. Your attitude must be that of Christ..." The Son is a formidable part of the Complete Being; however, He is not superior to His Father. I humbly believe that each of the three Entities of the Complete Being are not quite equivalent to one another, even though no one is more important than the other. If we were to symbolize the Entities with round circles, the Father's circle would be larger than those of the other two Entities; even though each Member has His own exceptional characteristics, which He funnels through to the Complete Being as a whole. The reason for this, is that the Father must be distinguished from the other two Entities, due to the fact that He is responsible for the existence and the continuance of the Complete Being. He remains the leader, and the other two Entities follow what He says. Just because the Father has a slightly bigger circle than those of the other two Entities, this does not signify that He is the most important Entity, however, it does signify that He is the decision-maker, and is in charge of His family; the Complete Being. The Father is the Delegator, and the Creator; the Son is the Savior, and the Final Judge; and The Holy Spirit is the Apostle, and Delivers the Sacred Gifts to each one of us. Each of the Entities is God, as all Three form God, due to their special attributes. Once He is God, He cannot become 1/3 God, however, as it is written, "Though he was in the form of God, he did not deem equality with God something to be grasped at." The Scripture informs us that His Son was not quite equal to, or on par with His Father, as I humbly believe that this is due to the submissiveness that His Son and The Holy Spirit show the Father; they remain obedient to Him. The Complete Being precisely and effectively functions through one of the Father's specific attributes, since He is the Delegator, who informs the other two Entities of their tasks, as all three Entities comprehend that this arrangement is best for the Complete Being. I can compare this arrangement to a father and his family. The father usually makes the most significant decisions for his family; therefore, even though he is not more important than any other member of his family, he still remains the final decision-maker. It was the Father, the Delegator, that sent His only Son down to earth; and it was the Father who told His Son, that He must endure death upon a cross for the life of our souls; and finally, it was the Father's will, which caused His Son to be baptized in the Jordan River by John the Baptizer. As it is written, Jesus says; "We must do this if we would fulfill all of God's demands." As we begin to deeply feel the Father's presence, as His Son did on earth, we should choose to reflect upon the existence, and presence of today, and not concern ourselves about the pressures of tomorrow, as we will have just enough time to pray for the distress and remorse of this day, before the clock has a chance to usher in the following day. The dark force could easily be capable of distracting our thinking, if we did not say our prayers daily; however, at times, we still get caught in a trap, since we instead decide to ponder the glamour and surprises which tomorrow may hold for us. We do not need to comprehend the unknowns of the future during the present, since this only leads to our confusion, and a sensation of heaviness upon our shoulders. As it is written, "Your heavenly Father knows all that you need. Seek first his kingship over you, his way of holiness, and all these things will be given to you besides. Enough, then, of worrying about tomorrow. Let tomorrow take care of itself. Today has troubles enough of its own."

Chapter 49: Holy Eucharist

Bread and wine are typical staples of sustenance, and in our houses of worship, the clergy is responsible for breathing vitality into the words His Son once verbalized, during the Last Supper. His Son is delivered from Heaven and becomes transfigured, as He is infused into the bread and wine, which has been given to us. The essence of His body and blood have now become prepared for us to gently consume. Why should we consume Jesus in the form of a piece of consecrated bread? His Essence, which we carefully consume, remains a powerful image, as it helps us to comprehend that His Son, genuinely lives within us. We use bread, since it is our staff of life, and it is plentiful; although more significantly, our staff of life, in this sense, can be perceived as a cane or even as the arm of a friend, on which we continue to lean. Jesus supports us, as we lean on Him throughout our own hardships, since He understands the meaning of physical and spiritual hardships, from being on earth. Physically, we need this bread to help sustain our bodies; especially if we live in a poor region. Spiritually, we need this consecrated bread, to sustain our souls. Jesus calls us to The Last Supper, in order to inform us that His essence is entirely within us, subsequent to swallowing the host, bread, or whatever food source is consecrated and used for this purpose. There are many people, who believe that His Son is not infused, nor disseminated into the bread of life, whenever our clergy offers this miracle to us. Many people declare that this sustenance, which helps us to recreate the words of The Last Supper, is more likely to be symbolic, than to be a reality. Jesus has indeed spoken in symbolic language before, however, the Last Supper took place during the most serious of times; a crucial time in His existence, when He was about to suffer death upon a cross. The message retained from Luke's Gospel is comprised of these words, as it is written, "Then, taking bread and giving thanks, he broke it and gave it to them saying: 'This is my body to be given up for you. Do this as a remembrance of me.'" When a member of the clergy says, "This is my body to be given up for you," this is the moment when Jesus' outer structure dies, as His body is shed, and He becomes the true essence of Himself, which enters our body cavity, and remains in our soul, subsequent to our consummation of the host/or bread. I believe that we should concentrate on the phraseology and meaning of the entire passage, instead of only focusing on a couple of words, which may alter the significance of the passage. I humbly believe that the message, from the Words spoken by Jesus at the Last Supper, can basically be viewed as a symbol, since we are meant to reflect upon the Last Supper and the crucifixion that follows; however, I genuinely believe that Jesus is inculcated within the host or bread, since His essence physically enters our body and spiritually lives within our soul. As it is written, Jesus explained to them: "I myself am the bread of life. No one who comes to me shall ever be hungry, no one who believes in me shall ever thirst." Therefore, when we receive our sustenance, we no longer find it necessary to search for any other means, by which we must be saved from the prince of darkness, who attempts to muddy our souls every chance he gets. This will take place, only if we truly have faith in His Words. Let us attempt to terminate our flesh-driven sins, since His Son has fulfilled the ultimate sacrifice for all of us. Let us never again neglect our Savior, and let us never forget how grateful we are to Him. We can show our love for His Son, by the actions we perform, and by the absolute faith, for which we continue to strive, forevermore.

Chapter 50: Internal vs. External Intentions

As it is written, "The affectation of an elaborate hairdress, the wearing of golden jewelry, or the donning of rich robes is not for you. Your adornment is rather the hidden character of the heart, expressed in the unfading beauty of a calm and gentle disposition. This is precious in God's eyes." "You husbands, too, must show consideration for those who share your lives. Treat women with respect as the weaker sex...If you do so, nothing will keep your prayers from being answered." These sound words of advice from Scripture may be executed, whether we are single or married. These quotes give us more than just a clue of how we, as women, are to conduct ourselves, including how our temperament should be simply, sweetly, and serenely, expressed to others. The Scripture reveals even more specifically, how we should act, while we are with our most intimate and exclusive relationship, while we are alive on earth. A most special and essential bond is formed, as we share our life and love, as husband and wife, or partner and partner. I humbly believe, that we may garner some relationship and marriage advice from these quotes. Our Higher Power does not consider the external beauty of a woman to be something special, since the jewelry and the clothes we wear is certainly not significant to Him. He does, however, assess and concern Himself with the internal intention of a woman, as He wishes for women to exist in a state of precious tranquility. Even if there is some internal strife between herself and her husband, she may be at peace enough, so that she does not have to worry about her emotions overriding her intellect, since she has learned to be tranquil, when her husband confronts her and unfortunately starts an argument. Due to her peace-filled spirit and the softened verbalizations of her non-confrontational words, she will have the ability to fully understand the merit of her husband's point of view, as she will give him time through her silence, to tell his side of the story without his anger flaring up. Reciprocally, he may wish to accommodate his wife's side of the story, while he remains silent, as well. So many times, during our marriages, however, we do not pay attention to each other's position during a dispute, since both of us feel that we should be listened to, before our partner speaks, as we both continue to converse at the same time, and nothing decisive is ever achieved. As we begin to think about all of this shouting and contentiousness, we may truly wish to give the other individual in the relationship, a chance to speak about his or her own thoughts in an atmosphere of serenity, as we should not battle against each other; otherwise this dispute will begin to grow louder and become wrought with confusion. We both know, however, at the very least, one of us will eventually deem it necessary to become calm and more malleable towards the other person's position, which will ultimately solve this dispute, peacefully. If we are totally cognizant, that we are correct during this argument, and the other person remains incorrect, let us politely give our partner a chance to speak his truth anyway, which we shall want to do in a peace-filled environment. In this way, we will teach him how our relationship can thrive, by learning how to speak gently, as he might even be the one to become adaptable towards our position, once the commencement of our next serious discussion begins. Let us prepare ourselves to enter into the Kingdom of our Higher Power, and let us approach our eternal life with great love, and appreciation for everything He has given us.

Chapter 51: Suicide

He who commits the tragic act of suicide, has often lived with one of the following unbearable situations: intractable pain, a grave illness, persistent emotional punishment, paralysis, or the feeling that everyone would be better off without him. I believe that he may come to the realization, that his tiresome and relentless suffering, seems as though it shall never conclude, as it may continue to be his daily norm. Simply said, he could not seem to subdue or silence the reason for his impending suicide, subsequent to attempting this feat many times over. As he envisions the coming years, he begins to contemplate on what his future may look like, which will most likely remain full of desperation, and therefore, he attempts to concentrate on how he will enact this permanent solution of death, so that it will end his continuous suffering. Suicide seems to be the final answer he has settled upon, although he had always been somewhat of an optimist, and therefore, there always seemed to be a whiff of hope, which wafted in and out of this desperate act of violence, he was willing to commit. Just then, he remembered one of his favorite quotes from Scripture, which said, "...We know that affliction makes for endurance, and endurance for tested virtue, and tested virtue for hope. And this hope will not leave us disappointed, because, the love of God has been poured out in our hearts through The Holy Spirit who has been given to us," as it is written. When we think of hope, we should acknowledge the great hope we have in our Higher Power and in His message, since there should be no one else that we choose to place our hope in, as hope translates into: confidence, trust, reassurance, and anticipation. Our Higher Power desires that our bond between His Son and ourselves, remains a strong one. We are all sinners, as we learn to lean upon His Son, when our circumstances and desires start to move in the wrong direction. Since he hopes that our Higher Power will present him with the strength to remain alive, because he does not really wish to die, this hope then becomes an important safety raft, sent to him by The Holy Spirit. Hope is eternal, as it remains a gift given to those who need encouragement. I understand through my intellect, that performing the desperate act of suicide is a sin, however, I cannot truly understand this within my soul, as my heart grieves for the individuals who commit suicide, since they were not able to remove themselves from the deep crevasse of emotional or physical pain. Our Father desires to protect and shield us from living with the dogma of the prince of darkness, and therefore, we cannot imagine that He would be upset with those of us who choose suicide as an alternative to our incomparable pain. I believe that prior to this individual's suicide, he will ask for forgiveness from our Higher Power and His Son, if he is indeed a Christian. If he is a non-Christian, then he shall follow the important precepts of the religion he practices. This scenario reminds me of the day, that Jesus was crucified, as two criminals hung on either side of Him. One of the criminals was blasphemous when he spoke to our Savior, and therefore simply died on his cross without any empathy from our Lord. The other criminal, however, stated, "Jesus, remember me when you enter upon your reign." And Jesus replied, "I assure you: this day you will be with me in paradise," as it is written. His Son maintains a clear and well-defined distinction between those who are humbled by Him, and those who are not. I do not wish to imply that the other criminal, who spoke blasphemously, will not arrive in Heaven at some other time, since I believe that he will, however, he shall not arrive there with Jesus and the other criminal, on the very same day of their demise. When we enter an afterlife, everything may seem crystal clear to us, however, this is not so on earth, and therefore, belief without absolute knowledge is the essential meaning of our faith. Each suicide is carefully judged by His Son's overflowing mercy, as His Son peers into, and delicately dissects the true genuineness of each person's soul, as He decides how long he will remain in the temporary premises without our Higher Power. During his time on earth, he may be delivered from his pain and/or illness by our Higher Power, however, in most cases, God allows this misery to continue, as the prince of darkness exercises his own free will. This pain, which is severely entrenched in this individual, even alters his tendencies to think normally, as he cannot see the fine details through his own glasses, which seemingly have the wrong prescription. This individual, therefore cannot understand, that suicide is tantamount to murder; just as the Sacred Scripture warns us. New medications for pain, especially for the suffering of physical and mental afflictions, continue to be discovered and furnished to many of us who need them, thereby giving him and other individuals, hope for the future. I believe that he anticipates that Jesus will be brimming with unconditional love and mercy for him, even though his suicide may continue to approach with every passing hour. I understand that I have not walked in this individual's shoes, however, I have had many experiences with agonizing migraine headaches, and therefore, I comprehend why someone could choose death over life, since my pain also becomes unbearable at times. There happens to be some resources for those who are coping with this issue, as I hope that our Higher Power will lead the individual and others to these life-changing encounters. I am sure that those of us who wish to end our own lives, have previously explored how to do this, as we tend to suffer horribly with the 'back and forth' of the distinct question of finality, and of the whole brave encounter of death. Let us recall that our Higher Power will never allow this individual to become embroiled in a circumstance, which he will not be capable of managing; and by managing, I do not mean by suicide. As it is written, "My brothers, count it pure joy when you are involved in every sort of trial." Since His Son died for us, I humbly believe that He will absolve those, who have sought suicide as an answer, since these individuals have lived such a tormented and cruel life. Let us pray in depth: for these particular souls who lived in complete distress, as they sought comfort while slowly entering the afterlife; and for the souls who have yet to make a final determination concerning this grave matter. The Holy Spirit promises to continue sending many saving rafts of hope to these tortured souls. Lastly, the protagonist I spoke of in this chapter, did not choose suicide after all.

Chapter 52: Let it go

I enjoy expressing love to my neighbors, especially my neighbors who happen to live on the fringes of society, since I am pleased with what I am able to give them. I exhibit this love by simply contributing a small amount of money to each of them daily, as my neighbors tend to seek-me-out, when I go for a walk downtown. I donate a few dollars to every indigent person I see, as each of them are homeless, which is unfortunately easy to recognize, since they wear tattered and soiled clothing. During one particular morning, I felt sincerely regretful, since I simply forgot my wallet at home. As a result, some of my neighbors hurled some unfortunate colloquialisms at me. I realized that these words were vengeful, however, I shall not allow the dark force, nor the disturbance of these colorful words, to enter my soul or my mind. I understand that words can be intense, as I used to form an emotional attachment to them when mean-spirited people used to taunt me, however, I simply refuse to do so anymore, as I continue to remind myself to 'cancel, cancel.' I feel more comfortable and at ease, as I endeavor to never again become enraged with what others say to me, since I will not allow these mean and discriminatory words to affect me again. Everyone is responsible for saying the words that they do, as we all have a free will which is given to us by our Higher Power, however, if unkind words are expressed, and someone uses the Lord's name in vain, this individual must be forgiven on earth or during the time they spend in the temporary premises, during an afterlife. I know that actions are more powerful than a few recklessly spoken words, however, I happen to have thin skin, so that every unkind word spoken my way, was similar to being pricked by a thorn bush. I must not allow these words to worry and entangle my soul, as I choose to discover my inner peace; a process which begins when I arrive home. I know that this process will help me to react in a calm manner. I attempt to remain tranquil, as I comprehend and remind myself, that words and their meanings are not as important as the actions

I perform. I choose the way I react to certain words and actions. During a conversation, it is very easy to pretend that a certain situation may be true. Words happen to easily flow into our minds, as well as out of our mouths, as many people may aim these particular words towards us, without much conscious reflection or expended energy. We know that our actions require more thought, more time, and more effort to fulfill, since the execution of our actions, are much more convincing than our words could ever be, and therefore, let us not place so much prominence on the spoken word. I can only transform who I am, since I do not have the ability to transform others. Please let me reply to their hideous words in such a way that I do not add stress to my life, or to the lives of the others who have just finished spewing these vile comments in my direction. I am now cognizant that I have transitioned into a person of substance, due to this new spiritual suit of armor which has been given to me, because of the prayers I have spoken in God's name, as He protects me from being disturbed. I understand that we are not being sprayed with vicious words when reading the Scripture, however, this is when we should pay close attention to each word we say or read, as some of our emotions may even come to the surface during our time with God and His Son. Let us not become too emotional when speaking and praying to God and His Son, as we should remain tranquil and not allow ourselves to let go of our thoughtful mind, and become uncontrollably emotional. When we speak about the Scripture, the word intent becomes important, since we can learn to wrap our minds around various, and sometimes unique interpretations of the Scripture. As we dissect the true intent, we find the significance of each passage, which begins with the blending of sacred words into sentences, which have been carefully written. Due to our various experiences, our intuition will nudge us towards the correct intent, of what a certain passage actually means. This may include the same passage we have probably read numerous times, however, whether we have read it for a tenth time or a fifteenth time, we may comprehend it in a slightly different manner, as it may presently help us to resolve some of our difficulties, since we can now relate to this passage. Actions are more important than words. As it is written, "Faith without works is dead." As it is written, "Why do you call me, 'Lord, Lord,' and not put into practice, what I teach you?" Both of these quotes resemble each other, since both of them imply, 'Actions speak louder than words.' As spiteful words discontinue to be significant in my life, I also wish to follow the same pathway concerning all malicious actions. In other words, it is necessary that I remove the urgency from the malevolent words I hear and the ill-spirited actions I see, as I become a person who begins to emotionally remove herself from the dramatic, as I feel calm, as well as easily portraying a person with a calm demeanor. Let us not allow the petty words and actions of others, to trouble or irritate us enough, so that our spirituality and the time we spend with our Higher Power, become tainted with adversity and discontent. If we ask our Higher Power for help, He will guide us and we will achieve our inner peace, while we refuse to listen to these mean-spirited words and hurtful actions towards us, ever again.

Chapter 53: Are We Always Correct?

The substantial burden we carry on our shoulders, due to our own expectation that we shall solve all of our problems on our own, is simply detrimental to our relationship with the Complete Being, and to the way we view ourselves. Some of us may have convinced ourselves, that we have the ability to solve any type of problem, without the aid of our Higher Power's help. At times, we solve these problems solely for the verbal accolades which are given to us by others, as we become the primary focus in our own pride-filled world of vanity. Our over-inflated egos must be stroked, each and every time we solve a problem. I humbly believe that we should resolve our problems for the genuine pleasure it gives us, or for the beauty of the logic which lives in the solution. For instance, in situations where other individuals attempt to help us, such as during a team project at our university, we simply, yet arrogantly inform our own team members, that we do not wish to listen to anyone else's ideas, and that we are not willing to share our information with the rest of our team, since we want to solve these problems on our own. Since we do not fully wish to participate in this task, we unfortunately do not allow ourselves to learn from our team members' good judgment and clever ideas, as we have yet to be made aware, that we do not have the ability to transcend the other members' intelligence. Wanting to always be right, we impede everyone else's skillful ideas, by refusing to listen and learn; instead, we solely allow our own mind to decipher the problem at hand. We may have correctly solved our exercise this time, however, we should not have continuously reiterated our completed answer in our own mind, as if no other piece of information had ever been as important, as our answer to this exercise problem. We rarely ever just simply listen to other individuals' notions and imaginations, since we believe that we can simply reflect upon our know-how, once again, as we will solve another one of our team's problems, when it becomes necessary. The unfortunate circumstance which comes from such thinking is that we also become closed-off from our Higher Power, since we can seemingly figure everything out, without His guidance; we feel as though we do not need His help for anything. As we stop learning from others, we will begin to be correct less often, as the only substance we will truly learn, is that our thinking will become stagnant and vapid. The truth of the matter is that we are not that smart, and have an unjustified claim in emoting the way we do. The significance of our emotional weariness is a result of the constant tension and nervousness that remains hidden behind our sense of superiority, which will eventually cover our mental prowess like glue, as it slows down our acumen. We will become stunted emotionally and intellectually, secondary to the exhaustion we possess within our own minds. Therefore, let us try to terminate this vanity and become a person, who is at ease with himself. Humility should be a part of everything we do, as humility translates into: lack of pride, submission, modesty, and meekness. Since we feel that we eclipse everyone, because we supposedly possess a 'superior cognitive ability;' we must live in a fantasy world of our own making. As it is written, "No man can serve two masters. He will either hate one and love the other or be attentive to one and despise the other," therefore, we cannot serve our ego and our Higher Power, both, and therefore, we must make a decision. As it is written, "In your prayer do not rattle on like the pagans. They think they will win a hearing by the sheer multiplication of words. Do not imitate them. Your Father knows what you need before you ask him." Our Higher Power does not wish to listen to clumsy and noisy prayers, since He is already aware of what we need. We must not assume that we continually transcend the mental acuity of others, since we are not mentally more capable or brighter than other individuals. We should understand that we must begin to act our own age, and begin to serve our Higher Power and His Son, instead of serving our own ego. As it is written, "Whenever you pray, go to your room, close your door, and pray to your Father in private. Then your Father, who sees what no man sees, will repay you." Some of us possess an inflated ego; especially if we allow others to observe how spiritual we can be. If we try to give the illusion that we pray more often than others do, we risk our intimate relationship with Him, therefore, let us pray to our Father in private. Once we comprehend that we do not necessarily need to seek attention from others, the desire to be correct all of the time, seems not to matter in comparison to the substance of His existing Truth. Let us put an end to this vanity; as it is written, "Then I saw that all toil and skillful work is the rivalry of one man for another. This also is vanity and a chase after wind;" as we all know, chasing after the wind is impossible, since it can never be caught. He also explains, that being vain is a waste of our time, even though some of us continue to chase it. We do not need vanity in our lives, since He loves all of us individually and unconditionally, as He has chosen to remain with each of us, forever. Accept yourself the way you are and enjoy the present moment, because God loves all of us equally; our I.Q. or our propensity to solve problems does not matter.

Chapter 54: Christianity is Born

His Son was born Jewish; however, He became the sole reason why this newly-found, life-giving faith called Christianity, started to develop. We became aware of God's Son, when individuals of all backgrounds first followed the star of David to the creche. Jesus is our God and our Savior. As He matured, He spoke to us regarding life-nourishing Truths, as He is the life-blood and the moral code from which the New Testament is derived. His activities were recorded on papyrus by the writings of just a few individuals, who had managed to capture the essence of His Words, and the performance of His actions. The Sacred Scripture was written from those writings. As it is written, "...Scripture has it: 'Not on bread alone is man to live but on every utterance that comes from the mouth of God.'" The New Testament will endure forever, as we continue to learn from these powerful scriptural writings, in which His Words and His life remain relevant to us, even now. Most writings of the New Testament were recorded no later than the year 120 A.D., however, there have been disputes with various religious scholars, as to the exact time these Books and Letters were written. Most scholars believe that a majority of the epistles and three of the Gospels were written from 50-90 A.D., and that a collection of Paul's Letters was written in the year 120 A.D. The Son has instructed us to live a fresh, yet mature life as we live His vital truth regarding: forgiveness, humility, love, and mercy. This new faith becomes His Son's new Covenant with us. As He gives each of us the proverbial key, it unlocks the door to an exceptional existence of forgiven indiscretions, so that our souls may one day live in Heaven. A segment of our Scripture, exhibits the love shown by our Higher Power's epic and noble creation of human beings. His consideration and great love for us was the reason for His Son's ultimate demise, as He became the Sacrificial Lamb. Jesus taught us that if we become quiet and prayerful, we will then have a moment of clarity, when we begin listening to Him. At times, however, I tend to be impatient with the Scripture, as the genuine meaning of the passages do not always enlighten me. This bit of negativity used to be the catalyst, which impeded my moment of clarity; however, I no longer allow this obstacle to function, as He grants me the ability to concentrate, when I read my Bible. Lately, I have come to understand the true meaning of the bread of life. I called upon His help, in order to experience and believe in this miracle, which occurs at mass every week. This miracle is the inculcation of His Son into the host, or bread; and wine, or juice. Now that His Son has granted us a faith, which concerns the mystery of the bread of life, I have the inclination to attend mass more often. His Son has promised to give all of us another moment in time, so that all indiscretions may be corrected, and all may be made right by asking for His forgiveness. I believe that this moment occurs as soon as we die, and enter the temporary premises. We should not be remiss in retaining such a great faith in His Son, as He also had to comprehend the quality of our faith in Him, since He accepted the crucifix for our benefit. Let us not disappoint Him, as we choose to keep trying our best to become the person who sins less, and listens to His Word more often.

Chapter 55: Joy

Our Higher Power wants us to appreciate the life He has given us. We have the ability to execute His desire, by carefully listening to our intuition, and choosing to righteously act upon what His Son declares to us. He also wishes for us to benefit from the joy, to which we have been given by The Holy Spirit, as He provides us with a message of hope, that we will utilize all of the beautiful gifts He has generously endowed to us. For example, The Holy Spirit creates and grants us contributions of all types, such as: kindness, grace, and patience. There are multiple degrees of joy that are created through our own perceptions, as we are now capable of only experiencing the most superficial sensations of this wondrous attribute, while we remain on earth. We will be fully engaged within the totality of this emotion, as it will reach the deepest recesses of our souls, when we understand joy through our new gifts of clarity and intensity. We will only experience this joy when our souls enter Heaven, with the Entities of the Complete Being. The manner in which we will feel complete contentment throughout our lives, happens when we start to understand what Jesus discloses to us, as we confirm our intuition through the trials we have been through. Let Him inform us, on how we must sacrifice and perform within the limits of our own moral obligations, so that we may remain attuned with our Higher Power and His Son. This performance then becomes a ramification of pure joy, which we shall indeed relish. The profoundness discovered within our joy, signifies that we have been perseverant in our pursuit of praying for our acceptance of veritable boundaries, as this continues to make my point about our morality. We will allow our minds, souls, and intuition, to then make sure that our ideas and our actions remain within God's limitations, as we ask for the gifts of patience and grace from The Holy Spirit. As it is written, "Be steadfast and persevering, my beloved brothers, fully engaged in the work of the Lord. You know that your toil is not in vain when it is done in the Lord." If we persevere in faith, and are completely engrossed in His work, our faith and our work will not be performed in any sort of trivial nor futile ways, since they were performed in the Lord. Why does Jesus concern Himself with our joy? I humbly believe that this answer is primarily due to the vast love He enjoys, as He envelops us within His unconditional love, and we become part of His flock, by heeding the words of 'the Good Shepherd,' as we take comfort in knowing that Jesus would never lead His sheep astray from what is right. Harmful behaviors, such as we find with infidelity and pride, are not healthy choices for us, as we become cognizant that our minds must soon battle against our own soul, for tranquility. I do not believe that we can attain true joy, prior to our soul's departure from this planet, as we are never fully at peace, since we continue to remain alive in the flesh, as our persistent temptations and enticements, continuously hunger for foods which sustain the flesh. We will only shed these cravings, when we enter an afterlife, which is within the Kingdom of the Complete Being. Let us remember that joy is abundantly available to us, through our relationship with our Higher Power and His Son. As we willingly follow His Son's teachings, we intimately pursue a most satisfying, and a most joyful relationship with Him, as this connection is responsible for His love insulating our love.

Chapter 56: Why Worry?

Why do we deem it necessary to speak and act differently than our genuine self, just so that others will pay closer attention to us in a group setting? We create these moments for ourselves, as we interrupt conversations, and at times act foolishly, in order for others to take notice of us. Why must we worry so much about this misplaced attention from others? This consideration from others should not be so significant to us, however, it truly becomes important to the individuals within the group, as we have taken an opportunity to disclose how we feel about the subject we are discussing, by consulting our new intrinsic identity. The group tries to understand who we are; however, we do not quite understand this identity ourselves. Why should we worry, and start to act out of sorts, due to our necessity for attention in this dynamic? What we should do instead, is to simply pray from our soul, which in concert with a willing mind, shall give us the desire to love and treat others well, as we should give the others the genuineness of ourselves; not someone who we think they would rather be around. Our life should always reflect that we are interested in the comfort of others, and not so interested in some misguided attention for ourselves. We should not necessarily concern ourselves with our shallow desires, since life should become more about our neighbors, and less about ourselves. Since we tend to think on such a limited scale, let us not become our mind's only protagonist, but let us exist with, and live beside a significant series of characters, which we call our neighbors. We recognize that every one of us is just as important as the next, due to God's impartial and equal love for each of us. We should never again worry about the petty things which matter so very much to us, since our Higher Power declares that we should keep our eyes focused on our love for the Entities and our neighbors. Due to the busy life we lead, it may seem as though we do not have a sufficient amount of time to connect with our Higher Power and His Son, and therefore, the prince of darkness may start to plan his devious workings within our minds, so that we begin to forsake His Son in prayer and in everything we do. Therefore, His Son says, "Come to me, all you who are weary and find life burdensome, and I will refresh you. Take my yoke upon your shoulders and learn from me, for I am gentle and humble of heart. Your souls will find rest, for my yoke is easy and my burden light," as it is written. We tend to worry about circumstances we cannot change, as this causes us great strain and our centeredness to be disturbed, therefore, let us communicate with our Higher Power and His Son, as these Entities will grant us peace of mind. We also tend to worry about the circumstances of our lives on earth, since we see them as being so very important, however, let us try to comprehend the breadth of the ever-expanding universe, where each one of us is a particle of miniscule proportion, which belongs to the overall immenseness of our surroundings, as the cosmos runs billions upon billions of light years away, in every direction imaginable. Subsequent to this information, the circumstances in our lives seem not to matter so much. Let us pry our minds open to something more interesting, more abundant, and loftier than just ourselves, as most of us feel as though we are the center of the universe, and other people merely appear as extras in our movie. Even though we are merely a speck of dust floating in the cosmic wind, we remain cognizant that we can make a difference in other people's lives, simply by praying for them. We now hope to realize that we do not sit at the center of our own universe, or even of our own life, as He is the One who sits at the center of each of our lives. We need not worry about the things of this world, since our souls will in turn be blessed, and our burdens shall be eased, as we recognize that worry only blocks our minds, and harms our intellect. We may be waiting for our Higher Power to answer one of our specific prayers, as we begin to worry about His response to our petition, however, this worry entombs our mind and spirit, so that the anxiety we feel when we worry, is proportional to the amount of care and concern we have developed for the response to this specific plea. During this time, our mind and spirit have not had the freedom to discuss other topics with our Higher Power, since we have been anticipating a favorable outcome from Him, regarding our previous prayer. This decision seems so important to us; yet so unimportant within the grand formula of our everlasting faith in our Higher Power. Let us terminate our worrisome behavior, so that we may return to the relaxation of His Son's love and mercy, even if we have not received our Higher Power's response to our plea, yet. Our worry will simply be washed away, when we choose to ignore our anxiety, and replace it with serenity, as there are several methods by which this can be accomplished. Presently, let us pursue a life of inner peace, as we choose to follow His Son, who has promised us that our soul, which is our essence, shall help us to become newly invigorated, as we enter our eternal reward, with the Entities of the Complete Being.

Chapter 57: Façade of Pleasantries/Authenticity

If we begin expressing niceties to one another, and treating each other in a kind manner, even though we do not truly like each other, then we are indeed, imposters, however, even if we do not care for the other person in the equation, let us open our proverbial eyes, as we may begin to learn some pleasing information about this other individual. The problem remains that we have a difficult time liking or loving someone else, since we only tend to concentrate on the other person's faults and frailties, which makes us feel, as if we are better than the other person. This problem of truly not liking someone else, has more to do with our errant personality, than with the other individual's quirkiness. Let us, therefore, communicate this inquiry to our Higher Power, as He will guide us and fulfill our desire for some assistance, as we may begin to love our neighbors as we love ourselves. Placing an emotional façade between ourselves and someone else, causes us not to care, as our refusal to be genuine with each other, is the work of the prince of darkness. When we use our façade of pleasantries, we both exhibit absolute deception. Maybe this problem illustrates that we do not like ourselves, and as a result, we cannot like anyone else, in turn. It may also illustrate, that we simply do not care enough for our neighbor, to be genuine with him. This facade blocks our true emotions from appearing, as we begin to uncomfortably speak about insignificant matters, to each other. Both of us endeavor to plaster a tired half-smile onto our face, since neither of us is really content with the other. We should attempt to be more genuine, as we might even find that we start to respect and like our neighbor, much more than we had originally thought. Being friendly and kind with one another is pleasing and the right direction for both of us to take, and therefore, let us attempt to sincerely feel this way. The love of our neighbor begins within our own minds, and it all starts with how we view life in general. I do not believe that we should flit from person to person, as if we were a butterfly, and use our façade of pleasantries, while we complement our neighbors; these are complements which are dripping with lies. We should not continue to show how shallow we are, since we comprehend that these complements are simply not warranted. There exists an entity, who exhibits kindness and wraps us in his niceties, as he desires our willingness to do what he says, however, let us remain vigilant, as he contacts and appeals to our intuition in a friendly and controlled manner. This entity hides his true identity from us, and is aware that he will never be allowed into Heaven. I am referring to the prince of darkness, who entices us, as he contacts us in a pleasant manner, so that he may secure our attention, while he communicates with our consciousness and subconsciousness. Which quality would help us to become further intimate with His Son since we need more of His help? I believe that we simply need to do some work; as these are actions, for which we do not have to maintain a great physical strength. When we are called upon to execute various actions on His behalf, we will demonstrate to His Son that we sincerely love and honor Him. We must be willing to change ourselves enough, to follow His Word. This certainly reminds me of all the wondrous works that Saint Teresa of Kolkata continued to perform, even as she became older and more ill. She certainly was not strong physically, however, she gathered all of her mental and physical prowess in order to aid the indigent with great fervor. She assisted them, as their spirits remained malleable due to her teachings, and therefore, she could help them understand the Word; she also hoped to heal these same individuals, with food and medicine. We do not have to perform volunteer work; however, we can do smaller things within our circle of friends and family, that will help to make their lives easier. His Son will aid us with the work we should do. We are cognizant that His Son did exist as a living being, and had firmly stepped into this world approximately two thousand years ago, as people of that era would speak to and touch Him, as He came to earth in order to complete a body of work, which was of unimaginable proportion. As it is written, "It was not by way of cleverly concocted myths, that we taught you about the coming in power of our Lord Jesus Christ, for we were eyewitnesses of his sovereign majesty. He received glory and praise from

God the Father when that unique declaration came to Him out of the majestic splendor: 'This is my beloved Son, on whom my favor rests.'" Therefore, since His Son had always maintained His authenticity when using His Words and actions, let us also be genuine with our brothers and sisters, who need us at critical times in their lives, as each of us may fulfill His work, and be pleased with our actions. Let us become a real and accountable volunteer, when we possess the ability to help others in His name, as we pray that we may become closer to Him, and remain confident in whom He is as our Savior. During the final judgment, as it is written, "... 'Come. You have my Father's blessing! Inherit the kingdom prepared for you from the creation of the world. For I was hungry and you gave me food, I was thirsty and you gave me drink. I was a stranger and you welcomed me, naked and you clothed me.' Then the just will ask him: 'Lord, when did we see you hungry and feed you or see you thirsty and give you drink? When did we welcome you away from home or clothe you in your nakedness? When did we visit you when you were ill or in prison? The king will answer them: 'I assure you, as often as you did it for one of my least brothers, you did it for me...'"

Chapter 58: Addiction

Are you currently addicted to anything or anyone? The word addiction translates into 'being a slave to …,' for if we have become a slave to a person, a particular substance, or a behavior, and we attempt to function without the source of our addiction, then this will indeed trigger some intense withdrawal symptoms, which will manifest themselves physiologically, emotionally, and psychologically. As it is written, "You must realize that, when you offer yourselves to someone as obedient slaves, you are the slaves of the one you obey, whether yours is slavery of sin, which leads to death, or of obedience, which leads to justice." Addictions consume our precious time, as we conduct ourselves within the manner, that the prince of darkness strongly desires, since he transforms himself and slips into our consciousness and demeanor, as we become spiritually debilitated. Even though it is clear to us that we are weakened by a harmful addiction, we are willing to squander all of our waking moments, while we continue to focus only on our addiction. The only question in our mind is when can we catch our next fix? This addiction compels us to think and react in such a detrimental manner, that it causes us to change whom we essentially are, as we become someone we do not recognize. It changes our personality, and even more profoundly, our soul, as we begin to accept and adapt to a bent reality of ourselves, and continue to go deeper and still deeper into our addiction. There can only be room enough for one master in our lives. Unfortunately, we presently experience this master as a substance we ingest, or as a behavior we execute, such as gambling, which forces us to lose ourselves within the powerful realm of addiction. Those of us who are addicted, must surely feel the continuous call for what we deem is our necessary evil, as it teases us to seek out and take more of the substance, for which we care so deeply. Our substance becomes more significant than the distant relationship we currently have with our Higher Power, as we simply cannot turn away from our addiction, and say the words, 'cancel, cancel.' We knowingly continue to impede our relationship, and more specifically our communication with our Higher Power, as the ability to see Him in our mind is almost nonexistent, as He appears as a remote Entity from us now, since we have not spent any time with Him lately. We harbor feelings of guilt and loneliness; however, we still continue onward, utilizing our drug of choice for the immediate gratification it provides us, rather than choosing to forge ahead, by building a stronger relationship with Him. The effect of the chemical feels wonderfully intense for a few moments, however, when the high disappears, the identical issues from which we had escaped, all come rushing back into our consciousness, as this becomes a never-ending cycle. The Entities of the Complete Being assist us in the battle for our soul, and remain within us at all times. Our Higher Power strongly desires for us to turn towards Him, while turning away from our addiction. If He senses there is a kernel of faith left within us, He will then help us to fight the sensations, which we possess for these useless cravings, and retaliate against the dark force for the grasp of our soul. This can become our miracle if we yearn for it, as good shall conquer evil, however, we will also need the assistance from others in the form of professional help, in order to escape our drug of choice on a long-term basis. If we succeed in overcoming our faux passion, our true passion will later be revealed to us, as our reasoning will begin to clear-up from the substance we have overly ingested. We would greatly appreciate a conclusion to this tiresome portion of our lives, so that we may commence to progressively gain some sanity, back into our lives. This will be accomplished through familiarizing ourselves with a rehabilitation center for our respective addiction, so that we may start to pray and revel in the pure love of our Higher Power, once more. Being aware enough to affiliate ourselves with a rehab center, especially for those of us who have been using chemicals for a long span of time, is extremely significant, since we know that we cannot negate the addiction on our own. We will need resources which are only available at the fingertips of the counselors and doctors at the center we choose. Even though we are at the beginning of the healing process, we are certainly ready to remedy this unfortunate situation. I urge us to enter into the center with purpose, and therefore not allow ourselves to become lost in the rehab rhetoric at first, since we shall surely suffer a lapse of understanding when we first enter, as this is the result of our brain remaining in a chemical haze, which lasts approximately one week. Let us request that our Higher Power assist us, especially through the first week, so that we may eventually grasp and comprehend what is being taught by the staff at the center. As we come out of our self-induced fog and rejoin reality, our Higher Power becomes closer, and still closer in our minds, as He has not been this close for a long while. Since we have been praying to Him lately, the wall between us is weakening bit by bit, as we can now see and experience Him in all of His mercy, benevolence, and perfection. Once again, we begin to feel His security, and warm love, just as we had prior to using these harmful chemicals. With our angel of protection, our intrinsic spirit, and the Spirits of the Entities of the Complete Being, we can beat this deceptive addiction, and never be fooled again. As it is written, "Just as formerly you enslaved your bodies to impurity and licentiousness for their degradation, make them now the servants of justice for their sanctification."

Chapter 59: Trustworthiness

The term trustworthy can be translated into the following three words: dependable, credible, and responsible. Whosoever possesses this comprehensive quality, is an individual of good moral character. If we are indeed trustworthy, it is due to a source of sustained integrity and a certain maturity of spirit, which was originally given to us by The Holy Spirit. One day, I headed off to work, on what began as a normal day. As I arrived at my desk, an acquaintance of mine walked towards me and asked me to go to the cafeteria with her, since she had not eaten that morning. I agreed, and so we secured a table in the lunch room, as she ate some fruit. All of a sudden, I heard a high-pitched squeak coming from someone occupying the adjacent table, as I saw someone choking in distress; everyone near her started to shout for help. I began to briskly move towards the lady in distress, and I was successfully able to perform the Heimlich maneuver on her; what a surreal experience. The morning after, that same lady came to thank me once again, as she revealed to me that she had an out of body experience during her choking episode. She further explained to me that she was not religious, however, she had been wanting to learn something about God. She asked me if I was religious, and if I could help her affect this change. I told her that our Higher Power was a living Entity, and He would very much appreciate, and very much love to maintain a relationship with her. I disclosed, that God had been waiting to hear her speak those very words, for a long time. I invited her to mass with me, however, I made it clear that I was a Catholic, and there were numerous other religions with which she could delve into and inspect, as I mentioned that she would be most fulfilled, by simply choosing any of the Christian religions. Also, I shared with her that she should purchase a Bible, and should become a student of the Bible; preferably in a Bible class, or with others, who know the Bible well. I had also declared, that she should express her prayers conversationally with the Entities, and their gentle response to her prayers will come through her intuition. I stated that, 'we must remain silent and wait for His reply.' I believe that her curiosity regarding how to go about learning the wishes of our Higher Power, was originally placed in her thoughts by The Holy Spirit. She then asked me, 'What does spirituality mean?' I answered her in the best way that I could, by explaining that spirituality has many meanings, however, not exclusive to: being with the Divine, retaining a natural curiosity regarding celestial matters, feeling our innate love for our Higher Power, conversing with Him and the Entities, forming an intent when reading Scripture, and lastly, it can signify an ethereal quality about a living Entity. She mentioned to me that she felt, as if her intuition was leading her mind towards something new and significant; therefore, if we are given the gift of being a trustworthy mentor, let us carefully and gently lead as a mentor, as we immediately ask the spiritual student to take charge of her own prayers to the Almighty, since prayer is the concept which is most significant at this time. It is of utter importance, that we, as mentors, have a degree of knowledge regarding what, why, and how we came to feel about a number of many spiritual subjects, since this individual will continue to ask us for answers to complex spiritual questions. I pray that whoever she encounters, friend or family member, that they will become a catalyst to affect her situation in the positive direction, as they will support her curiosity and her intuition. She feels comfortable enough with me, as her trustworthy servant, so that I may be dependable and responsible enough to guide and advise her, during this time of her spiritual awakening. Thank you, Father in Heaven, for bestowing this most formidable challenge upon me; as I have now become her newly appointed spiritual counselor. I believe that I am capable of counseling her on a new spiritual journey, and explaining how ultimately significant her Bible will soon become, as this will help her to progress further when she moves her spirituality forward, and begins to form her nascent, yet unique love of our Higher Power. I began to read two Bible verses to her this day, since I carry a small Bible in my purse. As it is written, "Everyone who calls on the name of the Lord will be saved," and as it is written, "I have set the Lord ever before me, with Him at my right hand I shall not be disturbed…You have shown me the paths of life;

you will fill me with joy in your presence." Let us recall that true happiness is discovered through the significant time we spend with our Higher Power and His Son, as He begins to reveal Himself to us, ever so slightly and slowly. Let us lead the life in which our Higher Power and His Son wish us to live, as we will always feel content in the knowledge that His Son will always be with us. What a rich history of love, mercy, kindness, and joy which we experience within our lives, as both the Old and New Testaments are woven into an undeniably beautiful love story, as the Father, the Son, and The Holy Spirit possess a tenderness, affection, and unconditional love, for each of us. As it is written, "For I am certain that neither death nor life, neither angels nor principalities, neither the present nor the future, nor powers, neither height nor depth nor any other creature, will be able to separate us from the love of God that comes to us in Christ Jesus, our Lord." She will now become part of this immense and undeniably wondrous legacy. I feel the excitement brewing within my soul.

Chapter 60: Good and Evil

We now know that our Higher Power created, and is responsible for everything within the cosmos and beyond, and for all types of life on this earth. Subsequent to creating us, our Higher Power made completely sure that our souls would depart to each of our earthen vessels. This task was accomplished by His delicate hand, which placed each of our souls into our human bodies, at the moment our mothers gave birth to us. I always wondered why He refused to sustain the life of our souls in Heaven, where we would have been a continuous source of intimate companionship and enjoyment for Him, instead of placing each one of the souls He created, into an infant of this world. Let us affirm that when our human bodies received our soul at birth, we would understand that this mutually satisfying creation between God and human, became a blessing, since we now had all of the intuitive and discriminating abilities, which would eventually help us to differentiate what was right and what was wrong, as our morals were indeed vital to a successful pathway towards our final adjudication. Our Higher Power did not create our human bodies as immoral beings; however, it was the prince of darkness, who was responsible for infiltrating our humanity, prior to his enticements, and therefore, the more we sinned, the more corrupt our souls became. Our bodies are responsible for causing the transgressions for which our soul must counteract, as we continue to request Jesus' forgiveness. If we could only focus on what is innately important to us, instead of what gives us fleeting moments of pleasure, we would sin much less often; this is why our communication with the Complete Being is so essential to each of our souls, which live within our earthen vessels. Since our Higher Power saw that too many of His humans were choosing evil over good, He decided to give us the ability to request His Son's absolution, subsequent to His demise and Ascension. As a result, our Higher Power was able to nourish and observe numerous souls, which continued to be gently handled and gently carried into Heaven, as Jesus saved multitudes of souls by the Words He spoke, and by the action of His death. There will always be an inner battle between our soul and the tangled web of earthly pleasures we simply delve into, and therefore, let us remember that we would have been struggling for the love of the three Entities, while we remained in the temporary premises, if it were not for our Higher Power's great love for each of us, as He sent His only Son to earth to save us from time in the temporary premises, as He continues to forgive our trespasses. Since His Son died so that our souls could live with our Higher Power, we gained an incomparable afterlife in Heaven, where each of our souls will enter with a pure and sinless innocence, after their visit to the temporary premises. At a certain point, we must choose a way of life, just as we must choose His Son as our Savior. As we recall, Adam and Eve chose evil first, and chose God later. God allowed this to occur, since at times, it is necessary that He tests each of us regarding who and what we truly wish for; by either choosing our Higher Power, or choosing the prince of darkness. When we were first conceived in His mind, I have to believe that He wanted us to genuinely and properly act upon what He said, even though the dark force remained in our company. When humans were originally created, He made a certain demand of Adam and Eve, as our Higher Power must have known that they would fail the challenge presented to them. Even at the very beginning of time, our Higher Power discovered that man's love and respect for His Creator, was simply not enough to abate Adam and Eve's commission of their first sin. God had to place the tree of knowledge in the garden of Eden, otherwise, Adam and Eve could not have utilized their free will, which was used to eat the forbidden fruit. This was a true test. Listening to our Higher Power's Words would have been very easy, if we only had one choice; however, there must be good and evil in the world, as well as a healthy dose of free will, for us to show Him how much we genuinely love and respect Him. We should inhibit the evil in our lives, and instead, choose virtue; that way we choose to remain with God, as we fall further away from the prince of darkness. Very early on, in Scripture, our Higher Power realized that He would need His Son's assistance to save all of humanity from self-destruction. This information was first captured in Genesis 3.

As it is written, "I will put enmity between you and the woman, and between your offspring and hers..." The "woman" mentioned in the quote is the Virgin Mary; "you," is the prince of darkness; and "her offspring," is Jesus; enmity means hostility or hate. Jesus would need to save us from the prince of darkness, as God placed hatred for the prince of darkness, in the Virgin, and therefore, this hatred was carried down from generation to generation. Our Higher Power was not so content with His creation. As it is written, "When the Lord saw how great was man's wickedness on earth, and how no desire that his heart conceived was ever anything but evil, he regretted that he had made man on the earth, and his heart was grieved." Our Father in Heaven looked back with sorrow upon the day He created us, because our actions were our own fault. God's disappointment concerning His earthen vessels, was eventually transformed into sympathy and love many years later, since He realized that His greatest creation could simply not adhere to His wishes. After the Great Flood, I believe that our Higher Power had to compromise His own expectations, concerning man's virtue. As it is written, "...Never again will I doom the earth because of man, since the desires of man's heart are evil from the start; nor will I ever strike down all living beings, as I have done." Our Father in Heaven understood that we, as His transgressors, would repeat the same actions, as the generations that came before us. Our love for worldly circumstances, popular people, and possessions, universally reflect our support for this world, and not for His love, nor His glorious afterlife. Even though it is difficult to remain on a pathway of virtue, most of us attempt to execute His vision. As time passes, God learns to display His loving attitude for us even more, as this is beautifully demonstrated throughout Scripture; this begins to take place, when His Son is born to the Virgin Mary, in the New Testament. There is plenty of hope within our hearts and minds, as we shall want to show His Son how much He is appreciated and loved. He lives within each of us, even now, and therefore let us treat each other with a special love, since we support His Son's Essence within every one of our earthen vessels.

Catalog of Quotes

Chapter no.	Quote no.	Where to find Quote in Bible
1	1	1 Cor 13: 13
	2	1 Cor 13: 4-7
	3	Mt 24: 44, 42, 36
2	1	1 Cor 12: 4-6 / 2. Mt 18: 18
3	1	Gn 3: 22
4	1	Wis 1: 12, 13
	2	Wis 2: 18
	3	Rom 3: 28-30
	4	Wis 2: 23
	5	Wis 3: 1
	6	Is 56: 1
	7	Is 53: 12
	8	Mt 18: 18
5	No Quote	
6	1	Mt 25: 40
7	1	Mt 19: 14
	2	Mt 5: 8
8	1	Eph 6: 10-11
9	1	Lv 19: 18
10	1	1 Cor 10: 13
11	1	1 Pt 4: 12-14
	2	Lk 11: 24
12	1	Rom 9: 15-16
13	1	1 Jn 4: 18
	2	Eph 2: 8-9
14	1	Ps 90: 4
	2	2 Pt 3: 8
	3	Heb 13: 8
	4	Gn 2: 7
	5	Gn 2: 23
15	1	Mt 5: 39

	2	Phil 2: 3
16	1	Rom 3: 28
	2	Mt 16: 25
17	1	Mt 12: 32
	2	Acts 5: 3
	3	Lk 11: 15
18	1	Mt 6: 6
19	1	Gn 1: 27
	2	1 Cor 3: 16
20	1	Mt 7: 8
21	1	Mt 5: 8
	2	Mt 4: 6-7
22	1	Mt 5: 22
	2	Mt 5: 7
	3	Mt 6: 14
23	1	Mt 5: 44
	2	Mt 22: 39
24	1	Mt 17: 5
25	1	Mk 14: 36
26	1	Col 4: 2-6
27	No Quote	
28	1	Mt 26: 34-35
29	1	Mt 26: 41
30	1	Mt 16: 18, 19
	2	Mt 6: 14
	3	Mt 7: 1
31	1	Ex 20: 20
	2	Ex 24: 3
	3	Gn 3: 19
32	1	2 Cor 13: 13
	2	1 Cor 12: 7-11
	3	Jn 6: 63
33	1	Gal 5: 19-21
	2	Ps 51: 7
	3	Jb 14: 4-5

	4	Rom 5: 18-19
34	1	1 Tm 1: 15-16
	2	Ex 21: 23-25
	3	Mt 5: 39
35	1	Phil 4: 6-7
36	1	Gn 6: 5-7
	2	Lk 7: 31-32
37	1	Jn 8: 43-44
	2	Eph 4: 29
	3	Mt 26: 21-24
38	No Quote	
39	1	Zec 1: 10-11
	2	Heb 1: 13-14
	3	Ex 23: 20
40	1	Mt 7: 1-2
	2	Jn 5: 22-23
41	1	Phil 4: 13
	2	Rom 12: 9-11
42	1	1 Pt 4: 7-8
	2	2 Sam 7: 12-14
	3	Jas 4: 14
	4	Phil 2: 21
43	1	Mt 11: 29-30
44	1	Rom 6: 14, 15
	2	Mt 12: 36-37
	3	Rom 3: 28, 31
45	1	Jn 14: 9, 10
	2	Mt 10: 20
	3	Ps 90: 2
	4	Lk 10: 22
	5	Gal 3: 6-9
46	No Quote	
47	1	Mk 6: 55-56
	2	Jas 2: 26
	3	Mt 14: 31-33

48	1	Mt 23: 12
	2	Jn 13: 12-17
	3	Phil 2: 3-5
	4	Phil 2: 6
	5	Mt 3: 15
	6	Mt 6: 32-34
49	1	Jn 6: 35
	2	Lk 22: 19
50	1	1 Pt 3: 3-4
	2	1 Pt 3: 7
51	1	Rom 5: 3-5
	2	Lk 23: 42
	3	Jas 1: 2
52	1	Jas 2: 26
	2	Lk 6: 46
53	1	Mt 6: 24
	2	Mt 6: 7-8
	3	Mt 6: 6
	4	Eccl 4: 4
54	1	Mt 4: 4
55	1	1 Cor 15: 58
56	1	Mt 11: 28-30
57	1	2 Pt 1: 16-17
	2	Mt 25: 34-40
58	1	Rom 6: 16
	2	Rom 6: 19
59	1	Rom 10: 13
	2	Acts 2: 25, 28
	3	Rom 8: 38-39
60	1	Gn 3: 15
	2	Gn 6: 5-6
	3	Gn 8: 21

Author Biography

Nicole Quatela was a musician and a physician prior to the success she developed as a writer. She declares that writing is the stimulus she needs in order to fulfill herself spiritually. In writing this book, she discloses that God literally guided her mind and her pen, as He told her the answers to many of the questions she posed, when writing, *Peacefully Centered.*

Nicole enjoys spending time with her loving husband of twenty-eight years, as well as with her extended family. She has a very special bond with her cat of six years. Nicole will continue to write, as long as her Higher Power keeps her informed of what is truly important, which she believes starts with the communication we must all share with our Higher Power, His Son, and The Holy Spirit.